About the Author

Marshall Jefferson is known as one of the Godfathers of House Music. He is one of the original pioneers of House Music that originated in Chicago in the mid-80s. *Move Your Body (the House Music Anthem)* was released on Trax Records in 1986 and this introduced Marshall's music to the UK and contributed to the birth of Acid House and the Rave Culture of the Second Summer of Love.

Marshall has now been a producer and DJ for nearly forty years and has worked with the likes of Kym Mazelle, Ten City, Jesse Saunders and Ce Ce Rogers.

Marshall Jefferson: The Diary of a DJ

Marshall Jefferson and Ian Snowball

Marshall Jefferson: The Diary of a DJ

Olympia Publishers
London

www.olympiapublishers.com
OLYMPIA PAPERBACK EDITION

A CIP catalogue record for this title is
available from the British Library.

ISBN: 978-1-78830-398-9

First Published in 2019

Olympia Publishers
60 Cannon Street
London
EC4N 6NP

Printed in Great Britain

ROGER SANCHEZ

I was a young, up and coming DJ in New York when I first heard *Move Your Body* on the sound system of the Paradise Garage played by Larry Levan. I had just walked in from the locker room area to the dance floor when the bass and the strident piano riff hit me and I thought, "What in the world is this song?" I think Larry played it about four times that night and the next day I was in Vinyl Mania and Rock & Soul trying to hunt it down. That was my introduction to Marshall Jefferson. Soon afterwards, I picked up Jungle Wonz and loads of other floor fillers from Marshall and began paying attention to his rise. Years later, as a fellow producer and DJ, I met him in the UK during the explosion of American House music overseas and found him to be a humble and enthusiastic person and very passionate about the music. I have a lot of love for Marshall and can't wait to see what he does next!

CE CE ROGERS

Undeniably one of the Godfathers and innovators of this thing we call "House Music". But for me, the friendship, fellowship and brotherhood would be one of the highlights of my life. Don't know what life would have been for me without this brother coming through and shaking shit up! Congratulations Marshall Jefferson and thank you Ian Snowball for bringing this story to the world! Ce Ce Rogers

INTRO
RIDE THE RHYTHM
By Ian 'Snowy' Snowball

Over the years I had seen Marshall DJ several times, one particular night was when he did the DJ warm-up set for a Happy Monday's in London, but I hadn't actually met him in person. When the occasion did arise our meeting took place in the backstage area of a small music venue in Ramsgate, Kent. Nicky Brown, one of the original Centreforce DJs was also playing that night and he ushered me down into the room where Marshall was patiently riding out the time before attending to his set.

I entered the room to find Marshall slumped into a battered old leather sofa. He looked snug wrapped in his blue parka with fur-trimmed hood. He wore a baseball cap and he had headphones on. He really did look quite at home and very at ease.

Marshall looked up and greeted me with a huge warm smile. A handshake followed as I too plonked myself down on the sofa beside him. We had spoken a couple of months earlier. I was doing interviews for the book *Specific State '89* and

Marshall had happily agreed to be included in it. It had been a few days after that interview that I suggested to Marshall that he should write his autobiography and that I would love to help him put it together. I was over the moon when he agreed that it was a good idea and, with all of these sort of things, timely!

We chatted for a while, Nicky B also pitching in as we talked about Trax Records, the UK House music scene and for some reason the group Trouble Funk. We then finished up. I wanted to dance and I got the sense that Marshall just wanted to chill with his music before his set. We agreed to hook up soon.

Shortly after that Ramsgate gig Marshall and I did indeed hook up and made a start on his autobiography. More sessions followed and what thrilled me about helping Marshall with it was how excited I would feel as we approached another session. Out of all the books that I have been involved with there was something about Marshall's that always put a smile on my face.

What Marshall's autobio does is provide a history lesson in Chicago House music and how Marshall knows. As Marshall shared his stories with me about hanging out in clubs like the Warehouse, the Power Plant and the Music Box and with people like Ron Hardy, Frankie Knuckles and Jesse Saunders I found myself feeling in awe of the man. But as the book developed there was so much more that revealed itself. Marshall grew up in Chicago at a time when there wasn't a huge amount of inter-racial relationships. In his neighbourhood there were gangs, there the Black Panthers, there were gangsters. Marshall witnessed it all and how these things impacted on the kids in the neighbourhood and ultimately go on to shape the Chicago House scene.

There were times when Marshall and I were talking on the phone and something would come up that we needed some clarity on. He'd phone guys like Sleezy D or Curtis McClain to get the answers and I would listen in and think wow!

As Marshall's autobiography developed I learned so much more about him and his personality. I always found him to be friendly, willing, nothing was ever too much trouble. He always made me feel at ease and he talked openly and honestly. Every moment with Marshall was a pleasure.

This was also a man who I discovered had worked and collaborated with so many people. The list went on: Frankie Knuckles, Ten City, Ce Ce Rogers, Duran Duran. And then there were all the other projects that Marshall had been involved with: Jungle Wonz, On The House, and Hercules.

How can such a man as Marshall be described? Well words like pioneer, innovator, game changer all apply and I believe the Godfather of House is appropriate too.

When the House music anthem *Move Your Body* hit the radios, discos and clubs in the UK in 1986 it was part of a wave of just a handful of songs coming out of Chicago that heralded change. Marshall's song was like nothing us Brits had ever heard. That piano! Wow, that piano changed everything. And we danced and as more and more music flooded in from the States we danced even harder and we ended up dancing in fields and warehouses and we were having the time of our lives. Some thirty years plus years later we're still dancing and Marshall Jefferson is still making us dance.

In October (2018) I went up to spend a couple of days with Marshall. The intention was to do a final edit on the book and wrap a few things up. I drove up to Marshall's home in Manchester and parked up. As I get out of my motor I hear 'Hey Ian, what's up?' From that point on I feel welcomed and am made to feel at home. 'Are you hungry?' Not really, but we go and get some Kosher from a place nearby. We work on the book for a bit and then find ourselves heading off to the cinema to watch Venom. The past few hours had also been punctuated with Marshall having loudspeaker conversations with the likes of Carl Cox, Bam Bam, Paris Brighledge and Ce Ce Rogers. Later, once we'd returned from the movies, we retreat to Marshall's studio/office and he plays me some the songs from an album he's made with Sleezy D. I love it. It's proper acid from 87/88. Marshall notices that I'm enjoying the music and calls Sleezy up and we have a three-way conversation. What a day! Eventually I go to my bedroom that I share that night with a pair of Sleezy's trainers that he'd left at Marshall's on his last visit. I fall asleep thinking how days like these don't come around that often. I know my world is a better place because of having a dear friend in Marshall Jefferson.

While putting the book together Marshall told me many funny stories. I had the biggest smile spread across my face for hours at a time. At the end of one of our sessions, just after Marshall had been telling me about the times when he'd hung out with Frankie Knuckles he told me a story about a particular gig and this had to be included in his diary of a DJ.

Marshall: It was about 2001. The Balkan war with Milosevic was recently over. I was booked in Croatia by a guy calling himself Ivan Mastermix. We hit it off immediately and start joking and clowning. We get to the venue, an outdoor venue, and it's completely empty. I think the Croatian Football National team had a party the same night.

Ivan is a bit stressed and I tell him not to worry. I just play a set. Only thing though, is I'm playing on a new Pioneer mixer, the DJM 500. I no longer have to have two copies of the same record because it has built-in flanging. It also has awesome echo and delay effects, so I'm having an absolute ball. I'm doing just about every trick that the mixer had to offer and the five people that are at the event were really into it. I finish up and go back to Billericay, Essex where I was hanging most of the time.

About six months later I'm booked in Croatia again and I figure it's going to be more of the same. Nope. Apparently someone had recorded my set from the last time with me doing all the fancy tricks and not only were the bootleg cassettes selling in the stores, but it had spread all over Croatia and people were going crazy.

I was booked to play at a club called Aurora in Primosten. The club's capacity was about 1,000 and that night another 5,000 couldn't get in because they didn't get there early enough.

Me and Ivan pull up outside, see the huge crowd and I'm thinking "wtf is going on here?" I get out of the car and everyone starts cheering. I quickly figure out they recognize me because I'm probably the only black dude in the country.

Ivan gets security to help escort me into the club. There's no backstage area and people are cheering at me all the way to the DJ booth. Some serious Me fever going on here baby!

I get to the DJ booth and I'm welcomed by an eruption of screaming and yelling. They think I'm about to play but it's Ivan's turn to play first. They don't know what's coming. I'm about to blow the roof off of Primosten: everyone here is going to remember this as the best party they ever attended.

I'm one of the best there is and when the crowd is receptive, within seconds they have their hands in the air and screaming at the top of their lungs the rest of the night. When the crowd is this enthusiastic before I even play a single note it's pretty much carnage. It's going to be complete utter nirvana resulting in mass hysteria.

I think Ivan senses this and tells me to go on first. No way the crowd is going to patiently wait while I'm standing right there next to the decks, so I go on. Sure enough, I'm ripping it like I've never ripped it up before-and I've done some serious ripping up in my time.

The crowd is in an absolute frenzy and some girl comes up to me saying "I love you." I LOVE you. Extremely beautiful girl, she reminded me of Cindy Crawford. A little skinny for me but very pretty face. I didn't smell alcohol on her breath, thank god, but she was definitely on something, maybe ecstasy. She tells me her name, something I can barely hear above the noise and probably couldn't pronounce it even if I did hear it. I play some more and she's kissing me while I play when another beautiful girl comes up to me. She says the same thing "I love you I LOVE you!!!" She's shorter than the first but equally beautiful. Both are too skinny for me but I'm having a great time anyway.

While all this is going on I'm working that Pioneer mixer like no one has ever done before or since, and when I finished blowing the crowd into dance nirvana I still have the beautiful girls with me.

I take them back to the hotel and one of them immediately takes off her clothes as soon as she gets in my room. The other one follows suit and suddenly it hits me; I am 41 years old. I do not want to fuck two women and have a heart attack. I want to go to sleep. I have to figure a way out of this. So out of the blue I say "Let's make spiritual love." They look puzzled but we hop in the bed and start kissing, and I keep everything from the neck up. Anything below the neck is going to start something I'm not prepared to deal with.

We're kissing and kissing and I don't know if I got some of their ecstasy from kissing them, but I was feeling it man, I was in LOVE. It was so beautiful, so spiritual. I was floating in a sea of pure love.

It must have gone on for hours, because suddenly Ivan came into the room. We were sharing the room and music business convention dictated that if you see your boy with two women, one for him and one for me. Or both for him and both for me.

So Ivan takes off his clothes and he's ready to do the nasty, completely ruining my three hours of "spiritual love" training. The girls start shouting at Ivan in Croatian and things look like they're about to get out of hand when I shout at the top of my lungs "IVAN!" Then giving my best puppy dog look I say "We're in LOVE!" Ivan looks at me for a moment then shakes his head and starts laughing.

FOREWORDS
By Byron Stingily and Jazzy M

Just like the first words of Sugarhill Gang's *Rapper's Delight* signalled the beginning of a new genre of music named Hip-Hop, Marshall Jefferson is responsible for sounding the alarm that announced the party genre of music named "HOUSE"! *Move Your Body* also titled *The House Music Anthem*, boldly told the world "GOTTA HAVE HOUSE!" Over thirty years later you still "GOTTA HAVE HOUSE!"

Marshall Jefferson is a genius in several categories of multiple intelligences. He is skilled linguistically in his ability to write lyrics such as Ce Ce Rogers *Someday*, and Ten City's *Devotion*. Lyrically Marshall could transition from dance to soulful melodies reminiscent of Curtis Mayfield and Isaac Hayes. Marshall is genius in intrapersonal and interpersonal wisdom. He has a keen sense of how to evoke emotions and make connections with people. Most people who meet Marshall feel as if he has been their best friend for life! And, of course his musical abilities! Having witnessed Marshall create music was different from watching any other composer I have ever had the experience to watch first hand. Marshall created music mathematically. He put music together in many small pieces, like a puzzlemaker! I asked Marshall many times, "Hey man what are you doing? You know that does not go together." He would continue composing on his computer (Yamaha QX1), truncating, transposing keys and quantizing time. Marshall was the first person who I witnessed who turned knobs to create music. When he was all done, the end result would be dance floor masterpieces!

His music also captured his fun-loving spirit! Marshall is a walking party and his music exudes his love and joy for life and a good time! His musical influence still resonates in modern pop music to this day. His piano riffs, drum beats, and melodies are the foundation for Electronic Dance Music, which now host events that sellout football stadiums and plays for young crowds of hundreds of thousands of young people. He is one of the most influential musical influences of modern time, but he is arguably the most unsung musical geniuses of anytime. Marshall Jefferson is the Godfather of House Music. He is a producer, songwriter and DJ. Without Marshall Jefferson the world would not know the international sound of HOUSE as we do today! Byron Stingily:

"Lost in House Music Is where I wanna be, it's gonna set you free"

These lyrics ring as true today as they ever did back in 86. My first introduction with Marshall was through his music. The second was via transatlantic calls as both our enthusiastic characters could not contain themselves on new demos that Marshall would send to me.

My pioneering House music radio show was The Jacking Zone; it was a platform for Marshall's music, as well as others. It spurned a friendship that has lasted as long as House music itself. I felt extremely honoured to have been asked to write this foreword for Marshall's autobiography.

His early productions like Sleezy D's *I've Lost Control* was like nothing I'd ever heard before and was like a horse biting my ass shocking me to lose control. I think I termed it Punk House at the time but it was clearly a very early Acid House track way ahead of the game. Some of my favourite productions from Marshall were under the name Jungle Wonz, which was his collaboration with Harry Dennis (The It) on vocals, especially *The Jungle* and *Time Marches On*. They were massively inspirational to the House Music scene and were ahead of their time being early innovations of Deep House music, which started as far back as the mid 80s. So it's not a new sound, baby. A lot of these tracks could be found on early compilation LPs and boxed sets I did to spread the Marshall sound, plus I could not fail to mention his collaboration with Ce Ce Rogers (*Someday*) and his production and writing for the band Ten City which spanned two LPs.

When Marshall used to visit my record store The Vinyl Zone in Fulham London (although we are now vegan and vegetarian) I introduced him to a lamb shawarma and it still makes me laugh to remember the many times he would ring me from Chicago and ask me to post him one while he was in a call also talking to Byron Stingily (Ten City) who would be in Japan on tour at that time. Those days were a true innovation to say the least as well as very comical.

The man, his music and his positive energy through the last thirty years have helped shape the Electronic House music scene to what it is today. I herald Marshall Jefferson as a true innovator right there from the start of the Chicago House music scene and he's still travelling the world deejaying and spreading the gospel of House. It's definitely not over!

"Jump Street Man - B-Cause" Genius

Jazzy M - Godfather of UK House.

CHAPTER ONE

*Marshall Jefferson wrote and produced the anthem for which
we salute the dance floor all night long! A true pioneer, he is
one of the few that have been honest about House Music's true
origins, recognizing that there is always a beginning,
Marshall remains consistent in his homage to* On & On *as its
beginning, and inspiration to give DJs the opportunity to
spread the love all over the world.*
Jesse Saunders

I was born in Billings Hospital on 950 East 59th Street,
Chicago, September 19 1959. My dad was Marion Jefferson
and my mother was Wilma Huffman. Dad was born in Chicago
and his dad was half American Indian. Mom was a quarter
Indian and from Columbus Ohio. I have no idea how or when
they met, I've never asked. My parents named me Marshall
Julius Jefferson. Hell, I don't know why they chose those
names but I've always told myself the Julius related to Julius
Caesar. I was their first child and my brother Scott followed a
year after me. We've always been close and I consider him to
be the best brother in the entire world.

My dad was a cop with the Chicago Police Force. My dad had a partner called Don Cornelius. He left the force and went on to create, produce and host the music show *Soul Train*, which was a popular show for more than thirty years and during its time included all the great soul and R&B artists like Al Green, Marvin Gaye, The Supremes and The Temptations. *Soul Train* was born in Chicago and Chicagoans were proud of it. It was Cornelius who sold my parents my baby crib.

Despite having a demanding job my dad was around as often as he could be around. I mean he would come home on lunch breaks sometimes so that he could spend time with us. I don't know how he managed to do it but he did and that meant a lot to me and Scott.

It couldn't have been easy for my dad being a black cop in Chicago in the 1960s. I can only imagine that he had to deal with some horrible shit. The thing was my dad didn't bring any of it home, so we were clueless. To me my dad was a normal dad. A very nice man and he never lost his temper. I was aware that people in the neighbourhood respected him and often people would come and talk to him and ask advice. But it wouldn't just be advice. People would come knocking on the door when they needed a ride to the hospital or stuff like that. He cared about everyone and people saw that in him. My dad died of cancer in 1993 and he wasn't a famous man but a lot of people came to his funeral. At the ceremony, people I didn't know were getting up and saying things about my dad and how much of a great and caring man he had been. He had obviously touched a lot of people's lives in Chicago. My dad was the nicest man that I have ever met and I feel proud to have been able to call him my dad.

Before my dad was a cop he had been in the army and had served in World War Two. He was honourably discharged at the end of the War. During his time in the army he saw some shit. I didn't know about this as a kid but I did find out some stuff in my older years. There were issues about the roles of what black people could or couldn't do in the military. One job black people got lumped with was clearing up the dead bodies (somebody had to do that, right?) so I can only imagine the sea of death he may have witnessed. However, it was better than being on the front lines, dodging bullets, and he was able to come home. But he never talked about the War to me. I rarely heard him speak of it. He was very good at protecting his family from those horrors.

My early years were spent living and growing up in a neighbourhood that was rapidly changing. For a long time the city of Chicago had been the second most populated city in the United States, until Los Angeles passed us in the mid-80s. Chi-Town or the Windy City (the origins of this are unconfirmed and Chicago certainly isn't the windiest city in the US) has had its fair share of shame, surrendering and sacrifices. Chicagoans have survived much, including the Chicago gangster and the Great Depression years and to help them we had music; great music and great clubs where we could hear jazz, blues, R&B and soul and with it Chicago gave the world legendary people such as Louis Armstrong, Sam Cooke, Nat King Cole, Benny Goodman, Gene Krupa, Ramsey Lewis, Herbie Hancock, Curtis Mayfield, Dinah Washington and

Chaka Khan. In many ways these Chicago people and the jazz, blues and soul clubs that they performed in contributed to the birth of the first House music clubs and those pioneers that helped shaped what would become known as Chicago House Music in the mid-80s. Chicago will always be my home and I try to get back there, see my family and friends, walk the streets that I grew up around and feel the breeze as it blows across Lake Michigan as often as I can.

When my family moved into the neighbourhood we were the only black people on our block. By the time we left there were no white families. Our home was on West 91st and South Union Avenue, which was a short walk away from Princeton Park. At the time the block was still being built so this meant there was space.

It was a pretty wide street with houses opposite and beside us. Reverend Brady lived to the left of us and down the street there were the Lees, the Jacksons and the Yancys and Sammy Brown. Now Sammy was a kid who was a little older than us. Everybody probably grew up with a kid like Sammy. Sammy would tell us how he would walk over to the next block and kick all of their asses at the same time, and we would believe him.

The neighbourhood certainly had its characters and they weren't all savoury. There was one guy who was a known paedophile. The difference compared to today was that back then people didn't openly talk about stuff like that. When I was older I learnt that that man hit on so many people in the neighbourhood, including half of the local baseball team, which he coached. He really messed some people up. He was one sick motherfucker. I was oblivious to what he was but I remember my father going over to his house to talk to him. My dad obviously knew what he was and who he had hit on and he did his best to protect us. Basically my dad warned that paedophile to stay away from me, and he wasn't going to argue with my cop dad.

I only found out about that paedophile when I was about eleven years old. I went to my friend's house to see if he was home and wanting to come and hang out. I knocked the door but there was no answer so I went and looked through the basement window and I saw him doing the gay thing with someone and I was like 'What the fuck?' I couldn't really grasp what was happening but I had to tell someone so I told my brother and then I brought it to my dad and my dad basically educated me on something's that had been going on in the neighbourhood and this included the paedophile guy.

One thing my dad never allowed was sleepovers. He wouldn't allow me to have sleepovers at other people's homes and he wouldn't allow any kids to sleep at ours. This was him trying to protect me; which I didn't really understand fully at the time.

Despite the paedophile and the messed up kids we had our community and all the places that make a community what it is. We had our local stores like Henderson's on 89th Street and there was Hoaks 93rd and South Halsted. And back then people did seem to look out for one another and I had my friends. Two were Gregory and Dwayne Jackson. My parents knew and trusted their parents and Gregory and Dwayne were the only kids I was allowed to hang out with unsupervised.

Gregory and me were best friends but we'd fight all the time. Although we were best friends there was also an element of jealousy. Gregory and Dwayne's father was what they call sanctified; he was very religious and he laid down rules that his boys had to adhere to. Their home life was different to ours. For example Gregory and Dwayne couldn't watch television. But they loved coming to our house because when they did they'd plonk themselves down in front of the TV and watch it non stop.

One time, a couple of days after Christmas, Gregory and Dwayne came over to our house. Now they didn't celebrate Christmas the same way as us so they didn't get any toys, but Scott and me had all these new toys that we'd been given as presents. Gregory and Dwayne came over and I think Gregory came up with an epiphany or something because he grabbed a hammer and said "You know what's even more fun than playing with toys? Breaking them up!" He then started breaking all our toys with the hammer. He was really going for it and Dwayne started to laugh, now really laugh, hysterically. Then Dwayne joined in with breaking up the toys and it looked like they were having so much fun that I grabbed the hammer and started breaking up my own toys. Yes, I was that stupid and when my horrified mother found out we'd broken up all the toys that she'd spent her hard-earned money on, we got the ass-whoopin to end all ass whoopins. Child abuse? Hell no. When I see other kids telling their parents to fuck off in shopping malls, I'm good with it.

I got to know the streets in my area well. From a young age I had a paper route. Every morning I would go out, by myself, and deliver the papers. Once a week I would collect the money. I didn't ride a bike and toss newspapers onto people's lawns. I would've gotten yelled at quite frequently. I placed the papers right in front of everyone's door. It wasn't much but I had my own money and could buy stuff like comic books and candy.

Scott and I were very similar in lots of ways. We could both be pretty stupid. We could both be very naive at times but most of the time we were happy kids and just rolled along learning and having fun.

I went to a kindergarten near to our home. I forget the name of it now. But I do recall my mother taking me there and handing me over to some teachers and they would gather the kids up and put us all to sleep because they didn't want to be bothered.

The moments in between doing things like paper routes and going to kindergarten were spent with my immediate family and then the wider family. We were like a traditional American family where we'd get together at significant times like birthdays, weddings, funerals, Thanksgiving, Easter, Christmas, New Years and 4th July.

On these occasions I get to spend time with my two grandmothers (one was very sweet and the other whooped our asses), cousins, uncles and aunts and we had some really great times and I'm fortunate to have a bunch of fond memories. These memories perhaps don't extend to my mom's cooking. She had a hard time with the cooking, she couldn't cook for shit. I didn't hold it against her though because she was one of the early black career women and that was where she put in a great deal of her energy. She could pull off a lasagne; that was the one dish that she could make, but that was about it. We didn't mind but sometimes we did tease her and give her a hard time about it and call it prison food and at many family gatherings there'd be somebody shouting 'Oh no, not the lasagne!'

We had a dynamic within our family that needed to be managed. I mean there was my dad the cop and there was also my cousin Bobby Rush. Now Bobby was second command in the Black Panthers. In the 70s Bobby became a politician and that was his world. He even ran for Mayor of Chicago in the late 90s. But in 1968 he co-founded the Illinois Chapter of the Black Panthers and served as their defence minister. The years leading up to this Bobby had been involved in various civil rights movements and campaigns and non-violence projects, he'd also been an advocate of 'offensive violence against the power structure'. This stuff drove him on and because of it he hit difficult times too. He was a close friend of Fred Hampton who was the chairman of the Illinois Chapter of Black Panthers. In 1969 Hampton's apartment was raided by Chicago police officers and he was shot dead and soon after that Bobby's apartment was also raided. During the raid guns and marijuana were found and as a result he spent six months in prison. A couple of years after this Bobby became a born-again Christian and got heavily involved in politics, which he went on to make a career out of. Our family are very proud of him.

Because I had my dad, the cop and my cousin, a Black Panther leader, no one in the neighbourhood messed with Scott or me. If there was any conflict my dad would shut it off before I even knew what was happening. As the neighbourhood got blacker and more dangerous my dad took it upon himself to get to know the local gang leaders. I would always see my dad talking to the gang leaders about something, most times I would guess it wasn't about me and Scotty, but someone else in the neighbourhood that had asked him for help. He didn't threaten anyone ever, he just calmly and politely talked to them.

On the whole home life was pretty normal. Scott and I would play together, fight together, hang out together. We'd sit around watching television and it was watching it one day that I saw something amazing. I was only five years old and The Beatles performed live for the first time on American television. It was the *Ed Sullivan Show* on February 9 1964. The Beatles performing live was a big deal for many people, white and black and, at eight p.m. apparently, something like seventy-three million people tuned in and watched them play songs like *All My Loving*, *She Loves You* and *I Want To Hold Your Hand*. What I saw just blew me away. It was not so much their music that impressed me, but their presence. I watched, with eyes wide open, four funny-talking dudes from England whipping girls into a screaming frenzy. Something awesome was happening. I really don't understand why that left such an impression on me but it did and it's always remained with me as a vivid memory.

After seeing The Beatles I got into pop and rock music. I really liked The Monkees and when I was a bit older Jefferson Airplane, but this was also partly due to the Jefferson name connection. Jimi Hendrix I liked because he was black and Cream were also favourites of mine too. This wasn't something that my family shared. I mean I been brought up surrounded by the music that my parents liked, which was black music. Motown was played a lot at home and also records on the Atlantic label too. Aretha Franklin was a particular favourite of my parents. And, oh man, Lou Rawls was big in our house too. He was a Chicago man, raised in the projects in Chicago's South Side.

We had two record players at home. One was kept in the front living room and the other, a close and play record player, which us kids could mess around with and fuck up, could be found anywhere in the house.

Our home was immaculate. My mother kept the place very clean and tidy. She couldn't cook but she sure could clean. The house was always spotless and she took it upon herself to keep it this way. Because of this she did it all and never waited for me or Scott to clean up (and even if we did we'd only do a half-assed job anyway). This is probably why my brother and I are so messy now, we just never had to learn how to keep things clean. I always pay someone to clean now; I just can't get my head around it. Sheila cleans when I'm in the USA, but when I travel, thank god for hotels.

Along with my friends Gregory and Dwayne I had a bunch of others from the neighbourhood too. We were just middle-class kids doing kid stuff. We'd meet up and play street hockey or a game called Strike Out, which was kind of baseball-related where we'd draw a box onto a wall and have to try to hit the ball in the box and when you did, that counted as a strike. Touch football was a popular game to play and that could be fun. The girls would jump rope and do their thing and mostly everyone got along just like kids know how to.

There were other incidents in the neighbourhood too, tragic stuff. There was a guy called Bernie. He had a motorcycle but was involved in a crash. He hit a truck head on and the whole neighbourhood saw his crumpled body lying in the street. I saw his body too and the bike and I've never ever been on a motorcycle because of that.

We never ventured out of the neighbourhood much though. We never jumped on the subway and went on adventures. I didn't even go on a bus until I started going to high school. I just hadn't needed to use a bus before then. All my schools before high school had been within walking distance of my house, so I had just walked everywhere.

The only times I ever travelled outside of the neighbourhood was when we'd jump into my dad's car and go and visit family who were spread out across Chicago. But as a family we went on holidays. Every year we'd go away and when I was young we went on vacation every year to forty-eight of the fifty states in America. The only places we didn't get to were Alaska and Hawaii. My dad would rent a car and he'd drive across America. He'd do all the driving because my mom didn't drive. We'd stay in motels, my brother and me sharing one bed and my parents sharing the other. They were great times and I got to see so much of America.

We also went to Disney Land and Disney World. I remember there'd been a huge promotional campaign by Disney. It was everywhere. There were TV commercials all day every day. I can still recall hearing that Disney music as we approached Disney World. It was magical!

Even though we did get to go on vacation every year and my dad had a good job, I wasn't aware that we were pretty well off. Of course I know it now but back then I took it for granted. I was aware that there were less fortunate kids in the neighbourhood. There were poor families and there were the problems that come with poverty. But the position that we were in we never rubbed it in anyone's face. I'm grateful to my father for many things. He taught me all sorts of shit and one of those things he said to me and my brother was 'if you flaunt that you have something that someone else doesn't, they'll get jealous and they will hate you and they'll want to take away what you got, but they'll also want to destroy you.' That has always stuck with me, but I still unintentionally slip up I guess, because as soon as I tell someone I got something new, here comes someone else asking for a loan.

Another time my dad took me and Scott to a homeless shelter. The place was filled with all these drunks and drug addicts. My dad looked at us and said, 'The majority of the guys in here could be considered geniuses, they are not dumb people, but they think that they don't have to work to get what they want.' He was explaining to Scott and me that we could be smarter than anyone else in our class at school but if we didn't work to get what we wanted, we weren't going to get it and we could also end up in a homeless shelter. That experience horrified me and my brother but in time it started to make sense.

I remember my dad also saying to me, 'Listen, if you have a friend in trouble in a burning building, it's okay to go inside to try to save them. But if he starts grabbing onto stuff and dragging his feet and it becomes a problem, then you put him down and you get the hell out of there.' I've not always taken this advice on board and there have been times when I have tried to help friends, but it hasn't worked out.

My neighbourhood and Chicago had a lot to offer. We had our artists and writers and musicians and other people of note who went on to great things. One of those guys was Barack Obama. He once lived about four blocks away from me, on either Parnell or Normal, I forget which one. He also went to Trinity Church which was about five or six blocks away, next to Princeton Park.

Another guy who played a very important part in black Chicago history was Fred Hampton, the Black Panther. He'd go into the ghettos and the projects and he'd wake up black people at six a.m. and get them out doing calisthenics workouts like jumping jacks. Hampton was a leader and he could get black people to do things that other leaders like Malcolm X or Martin Luther King just couldn't do. Well maybe Malcolm X could've gotten them to do it, come to think of it, but he didn't. What Fred did though was scare the fuck out of white people in Chicago.

So, the Fred Hampton story relates to the history of House music. Hampton tried to unite all the black gangs in Chicago and stop them from fighting and killing one another. This of course was unacceptable in probably the most racially segregated city in America. Soon there was a conscious effort to break up what Hampton and the Black Panthers were doing, and everyone involved was either imprisoned or killed.

Hampton's Monroe Street apartment was raided by the Chicago Police Department on December 4 1969. Hampton was asleep in his bed with his fiancée who was also nine months' pregnant with their child. Shots were fired, two of which were fired at point-blank range into Hampton's head, killing him. Other Panthers were also in the apartment at the time and some were either killed, injured or arrested. My cousin Bobby called the incident an 'execution squad' and what followed was an in-depth investigation that addressed many issues relating to race, the police and the Panthers. The impact on the Chicago and US black community was massive. More than 5000 people attended Hampton's funeral and that speaks for itself.

It was only years later that I realised the events from that time were so important and what part it played in the development of House Music. There was a time when my father knew exactly who the neighbourhoods' gang leader was, and he would talk to him. The key was having a line of communication. When a conflict would come, many people would approach my dad to mediate, and a lot of situations were defused that way. When Chicago law enforcement saw Fred Hampton attempting to unite the gang, they panicked and set out to eradicate gang leadership. Within a year, most of the heavy hitters of gang leadership were either dead or in jail. What this did was destroy lines of communication, and gangs splintered into smaller groups until you had basically a different gang on every block. So no longer could you talk to one guy that was boss of a whole neighbourhood or even two, but you had to dodge bullets if you walked on the next block. This situation still exists today, which is why Spike Lee was able to make the movie *Chiraq*, because Chicago at one point had more gun murders and violence than Afghanistan over a ten year period.

By contrast, New York united their gangs under Hip Hop. They not only had control over their gangs, but at one point they told members to break dance instead of fight. The gangs threw parties, and if you cut up at a gang sponsored party, you may just get taken into a back room and your friends won't ever see you again. So a Hip Hop party was the safe party in New York.

Not so much in Chicago. Hip Hop party in Chicago you'll have metal detectors and pat downs and you'll still get shooting.

We, however, found a solution. The black kids found out that gay parties were always non-violent. Why? Because gangsters wouldn't go near them, and if any gangster *did* show up, they were there alone and on the down-low undercover tip just to have a good time. We quickly found out that playing European or sexually ambiguous music would also keep the gangsters away. Finally, we found that naming a party after the locally famous gay club called the Warehouse, shortened to "House" ensured that any gangsters in the area would run in the opposite direction when seeing "House" on the bill.

To this day, every party you see in Chicago that's a "House" party has no metal detectors, no pat downs, no searches, and you never have to worry about violence. The annual Chosen Few Picnic gets 60,000+ people and there's minimal security. People bring their kids and grandkids, and you never worry about violence of any kind. Music is the focus.

After the Fred Hampton incident my dad actually quit being a cop. He felt he had to after witnessing white cops celebrating Hampton's death. My dad's principles wouldn't allow him to continue to work as a cop in Chicago at that time.

It worked out for my dad because after he left the police department he became a parole officer. He was an amazing dude. He went back to school and got his master's degree and some years after that he became a prison psychologist. Back in those days prison psychologists would come and go fairly quickly – it wasn't an easy job and stress levels were high working in that field. My dad worked as a prison psychologist for twelve years. There was something familiar and natural about that work for him and he also knew some of the prisoners from when he'd been a cop and a parole officer. I think many of those guys respected my dad and didn't feel that they needed to mess with him.

My dad got along with everyone. I still have people come to me know and tell me things about my dad. Ce Ce Rogers, who I produced, met my dad twice. Now Ce Ce told me that my dad said something to him that made such an impact that he went back to school to get a degree. He got his degree and went on to become a school teacher. Another guy who met my dad was Byron Stingily of Ten City, who I also worked with, he went back to school too and got his degree and he is now a principle in a school.

I think people listened to my dad because he had advice to give. He also spoke softly and had a very gentle tone and this would calm people and hold their attention. He asked the right questions too and this made people think and reflect. He'd say to the guys who were making music 'Hey, music is a good thing, but what are you going to do if things don't work out for you?' My dad tried to encourage people to consider a back-up plan. I guess it's something that I didn't inherit from my dad because I can't get anyone to listen to me.

My mother was a career woman. She was a school teacher until 1976, when she got "saved" and got into religious television.

Certain memories are particularly strong. Another significant event that shocked the community and people in my neighbourhood was the assassination of Martin Luther King Jr. I can recall TV programmes getting interrupted by special announcements about what had happened. I tried to understand what was going on because I didn't actually know who Martin Luther King was. I was only nine years old and like the Black Panthers, King wasn't a part of my reality. My reality was playing out in the street and listening to The Monkees and The Beatles.

But King was a huge part of many people's reality and I remember hearing people screaming in the street. I went outside and my neighbours were yelling and crying and I was like 'What the hell's going on here?' I stood and watched all this unfold until my mother told me to come back inside the house. King's assassination on that April day in 68 was all over the news and brought up in every conversation. It wasn't until years later that I really understood who King was and what he was all about and how tragic he was murder was.

What did touch me was the moon landing in the summer of the following year. Watching Buzz Aldrin and Neil Armstrong land on the moon was an amazing thing. I think we all felt a part of it. Man, I even pretended to be an astronaut and climbed into the clothes dryer, closed the door and peered out of the round glass door as if I was looking out of one of the Apollo 11's windows. I guess that wasn't the safest thing to have done.

The build-up to the moon landing had been all over the TV for weeks and then there had been the take-off. I sat cross-legged in front of the TV and counted down with millions of other people – 10, 9, 8, 7, 6, 5, 4, 3, 2, 1 and boom. Yeah man, the take-off was big time. It was so exciting for a boy of my age.

So much pioneering stuff seemed to happen in the sixties and into the early seventies. I caught some of it, understood some of it and ignored most of it.

When I was thirteen I went to Lindblom High School on S. Wolcott Avenue. It was a massive building with eight tall Roman-style columns at the front entrance. It had a huge auditorium, gymnasiums and an impressive study hall. It was a well-established school that had been teaching students for fifty years by the time I started to attend. A few famous people passed through the school, athletes and so forth and Steve 'Silk' Hurley went there too. I was a few years before Steve, so I didn't know him at Lindblom, but his brother Michael was my hero. Every time I saw him he was with a different beautiful girl.

Lindblom was a technical high school that was meant to prepare students to enter vocations in industrial and skilled trades. Much of time at Lindblom was tough. I didn't get good grades. I had some really great teachers so it wasn't their fault – I just didn't connect with the classroom. But something happened to my IQ score in the fourth grade. One other guy and I were singled out as having very high IQs. That other guy, Steven Talbot, is an astrophysicist now. He got perfect grades and was a textbook genius. And then there was me. I didn't do any homework. When I got home from school I just wanted to hang out with my friends. I had no time for doing homework; a classic underachiever and fuck-up.

There was one teacher in fifth grade called Miss Schmidt and even though I didn't do my homework and almost flunked out, she passed me anyway because of my high IQ. I was also very distracted in fifth grade by Gabrielle Readus. I learned from an early age that I was a boob man and Gabrielle had double Ds when she was 10 years old. On top of that, I sat right behind her, so I was swooning and daydreaming all day every day. In the sixth grade we were graded on how much we knew and how well we did in tests. Homework had no bearing on grades so I was a superstar. In this grade, there was a teacher called Miss Whitley and man, she was fine. She was also an excellent teacher and graded you on how you did your schoolwork instead of how much schoolwork you did, so naturally I got straight As for the first time in my life in her class.

My next teacher was Miss Bryant and she was one of those teachers that judged you on how much homework you did. But I still wasn't doing my homework so I came really close to failing and being put back a year. Another thing about Miss Bryant was that she had the most gigantic boobs I had ever seen, even bigger than Gabrielle's. Sometimes she would catch me mid-daydream and I couldn't even talk.

My not doing brilliant in school didn't sit well with my mother, the school teacher, at all. Every report card I got meant ass-whooping time for me.

But I somehow made it to seventh grade despite coming dangerously close to flunking. What saved me was a math contest called the Math Down. I won it, Steven Tolbert came in second. Nobody could believe it, including me, and Miss Bryant was furious. She couldn't flunk the math champion, so I got away with skipping homework for a whole year.

High school is a time of experiences and learning and finding your own way. Like any school there was a mixture of good and bad apples and the two kind of exist side by side. At Lindblom we didn't have school uniforms – instead we wore our own clothes. My clothes were nerd clothes. Pants were either floods (too short) or water drinkers (too long). Shoes I really didn't give a fuck about. We didn't have Jordans back then. I suppose I could have bought nicer clothes, but by then I was addicted to comic books and records. It was noted by the other students and I had to find my ways to deal with that.

What I liked about high school was hanging out with my friends and we'd get up to all sorts of stuff. When we were a bit older we'd hang out and get high. That was fun.

Lindblom was located in a bad neighbourhood and a lot of shit went down there. The bulk of Chicago's murders occurred in the area surrounding Lindblom, which was Englewood.

My friends were characters. One of them was Leroy Fennell. Now for some reason he'd want to walk around the school every lunch time and I would go with him, along with some of the other nerds. During these walks we'd often get robbed. Guys from the neighbourhood would come onto the school premises and rob us of our bus fare money, which was thirty cents. What was interesting was that they would rob every single one of us except for Leroy. At the time we just thought Leroy was too cool for those guys to rob, but what we found out was that he had a relative in that neighbourhood and was setting our dumb asses up. It was only years after high school that the penny dropped.

Lindblom was about an hour's bus ride from where I lived. On school days I had to wake up early to make sure I had enough time to do my paper route, get myself ready and hop on the bus. School would finish at three and then I would head home.

My other friends from that period included Reggie Harman, Anthony Fernandez, Michael Wright, Kevin Clay and Mario Hudson. There was a girl that hung out with us whose name was Pamela Watts. Pamela liked me and had a bit of a crush on me. I liked her too and would protect her even though she was like six feet tall. It was a matter of I was going to be her boyfriend or she was going to kick my ass.

The other fun thing about school was the girls. Oh boy, the girls. There was one girl I was in love in called Gabrielle. She was much older than me, but my God she was something else. My first love's name was Esther but my first real girlfriend was Janine. I was nineteen when we started to see each other. Because I spent the majority of my time hanging with my crew I didn't have a lot of girlfriends. I just didn't seem to have time or the opportunity to hook up with them. Janine had a sister called Angie and my friend Derrick was seeing her. We were just kids so we'd be coming out from separate rooms and smell each other's fingers and stuff.

The unique thing about my crew with Reggie, Anthony and so on was that we all liked rock and roll. Even Leroy liked the same music as us, despite being born and bred in Englewood.

Rock and roll was the thing that bonded us together. We loved those records made by Elton John, David Bowie, Black Sabbath and Led Zeppelin. Because I had my paper round and was making some money, it meant that I could go and buy records.

Something did go wrong at school with my grades again because Lindblom didn't give a damn about my high IQ. I couldn't do homework even if I wanted to because I had after school jobs. And I definitely wouldn't have done homework even if I didn't work. My dad offered me a choice. I could either go to a school called Central YMCA and graduate on time, or I could stay in Lindblom and flunk out. I went to

Central YMCA and this meant a fresh start for me. Because of this I did manage to graduate on time.

Going to Central YMCA meant I had to leave a lot of my friends behind and that school was a different world altogether. At Central the teachers would allow us to smoke cigarettes in the class room. Central was set up in the early sixties to be a different type of school. At Central the teachers actually treated the students like human beings. The lessons were better too. We had music appreciation classes and the music teacher would play rock and roll music to us and this was right up my alley. That same teacher also took us to a classical music concert and I thought that was amazing.

There was a liquor store near Central and I would buy a bottle of something almost every day and spend my time in classes being drunk. This was really the beginning of my alcohol and substance abuse. I started washing and bussing dishes to get more money. This was a problem because alongside buying records, I could buy alcohol and substances too.

It was around this time that I got with my second bunch of friends which was Steve Hall, Derrick Harris, Calvin Powell and Bernard Howard. Dion Carter was also one of my favorite friends, but he didn't live in the same neighbourhood as the rest of us so we lost him after High School.

Bernard was pretty much the leader and a huge music aficionado. He always knew everything about every act in every genre first, and if Bernard gave his seal of approval you knew it was cool. Bernard lived two blocks away from me. We could use his place and we'd gather there every day and listen to mainly rock music, most of which was supplied by me because I was the only one with a job and the money. I was also the one who supplied the weed. Bernard's mother worked at the post office and would often do the graveyard shift.

Derrick Harris became known as Sleezy D and I made my first record with him. The song was called *I've Lost Control* which Trax Records issued in 1986. A lot of people say this was the first Acid House song but I'll get into that debate later on in the book.

Another guy in our crew was Calvin Powell. He was a really smart guy and pretty cool and he really liked his rock music. Calvin also had use of his parents' car and would get a lot of women. Hercules was Michael Smith, a big dude with the quickest wit I've ever heard; he should have been a comedian. There were also the Southall brothers – David and Beeny and this concluded our crew that would hook up, listen to music and get high.

Weed was our thing but there were other substances going around. I recall there being something called Mister Natural. It was a tiny pill with a little stick man etched into it. I don't really know what that drug was.

Acid was also easy to get hold of. At that time acid came in pills form rather than as a liquid or on blotter paper. Lysergic Acid Diethylamide or LSD had been central to the hippy and counter culture movement in the mid to late 60s. In the 60s it was often given names like Uncle Sid or Alice and then when it became fashionable again during the acid house period of the late 80s it had new names like microdots, Strawberry Fields or Window Panes.

Although the acid I took with my friends was a hallucinogen I never really had much of a hallucinogenic experience or trip with it. My friends would use the drug though and they would tell me about their 'trips' and the shit that they would be seeing.

Our substance intake was always accompanied with music and some of the most important records for us around that time were Led Zeppelin's *Physical Graffiti*. That was the album with songs like *Ten Years Gone, Houses of the* Holy and *Kashmir* on it. *Kashmir* can only be described as being epic.

There was *Close to the Edge* by YES that included the parts on side one: *The Solid Time of Change, Total Mass Retain, I Get Up, I Get Down* and *Seasons of Man*. Eighteen minutes of rock heaven. Elton John's *Goodbye Yellow Brick Road* with *Funeral For A Friend/ Love Lies Bleeding* on it, oh man! This album was very significant for me.

As a group Led Zeppelin was very important to me. I heard something in them that no one would be believe me when I told them. It was obvious to me but other people didn't seem to get it. Led Zeppelin sped up the tapes that they recorded on after their first album to make them sound like better musicians.

Their debut album simply called *Led Zeppelin* that they released in 1969 was recorded at normal speed. But *Led Zeppelin II* was sped up significantly. This can be evidenced in the *Song Remains the Same* album, which was their live album from concerts recorded at Madison Square Gardens in New York City. The concerts were also filmed and when you play the movie and the record side by side you can see the difference in the speeds. The movie footage is much slower. Led Zeppelin were legends, but they sped up the fucking tape man.

This understanding I had about Led Zep became significant for my own music career. When my music career started I was thinking about Led Zeppelin. I went to a music store and there was a guy in there selling what were called Yamaha QX1s, which was a sequencer. He told me that if I had one of those I could play keyboards like Stevie Wonder, even if I didn't know how to play at all. I was like 'Fuck, this is just what I have been looking for.' It was as if a light bulb went off in my head and I was like right, I can do this, I can get records out like Jesse Saunders.

I'm really excited and buying into the idea of taking one of them sequencers off of his hands and I ask him how much. He comes back with, 'It'll be three thousand dollars.' I'm like, 'Fuck, I haven't got three grand man!' but he asks me where I work and I told him that I worked at the post office; which at that time was a good job with benefits and a future; I mean email was nowhere in the picture. So, it was a matter of 'Hi, saying step right into my office' and he gave me a ten thousand dollar credit line.

Boom! I've got me a QX1 and I'm ready to go home. But then this guy says to me 'Hey, wait a minute, this is a sequencer, have you got a keyboard? You're going to need a keyboard. You don't want to have a sequencer without a keyboard do you?' to which I reply 'No, you're right' and then purchase a keyboard, too.

The guy then asks me what I want to do with my new QX1 and my new keyboard and I tell him that I want to do records. The guy next tells me that to do that I'd need a drum machine. I think about it and agree 'Yeah right, I do need a drum machine if I'm gonna make a record like Jesse Saunders.' So I now have a QX1, a Roland JX8P keyboard and 808 drum machine and I think I'm ready to go and make some House music. But then the guy tells me that to hear everything I would also need a mixer. I come back with, 'No man, I'm a DJ and I already have a mixer.' But he takes pleasure in telling me that what I have is a DJ's mixer and what I really need is a recording mixer. So I'm like, 'Yeah, I need a recording mixer to go with my QX1, my keyboard and my drum machine and I get the recording mixer too.' This is what I'm telling you, my whole life people tell me stuff and I believe them, just like back in the days when Gregory Jackson told me I should break up my own toys and shit. I've got numerous examples of me doing stupid shit.

I think I'm ready to leave the music store. I have everything I need. But no. I'm holding all these boxes and the guy then drops 'You'll also gonna need one of these' and he presents a Tascam Four Track portable studio. It was a four-track recorder. I put my boxes down and I guess he thought he'd hit the jackpot because then there was one more thing that he thought he couldn't get rid of. For one hundred and fifty dollars he told me I could be the owner of a TB 303. What the hell does that do, I ask? And the guy explains that the TB 303 will create bass lines for me. And I'm like 'Yeah, I wanna make bass lines.' So I throw in the 150 dollars and I have everything that I need.

I carry all this stuff home and my friends come over and they all say, 'What you gonna do with all that shit, Marshall?' I tell them that I'm going to make records and they all start laughing their asses off. Man, they talked about me for the next five hours, and a lot of people don't understand that when black people talk about you it's an art; I felt about two inches tall when they finished.

But you see before I had spent a dime on all that equipment I had been thinking about Led Zeppelin and how they sped up their records to make themselves sound like better musicians, well I had my QX1, I applied my mathematics that had seen me through my high school days and, with my new equipment, I recorded a line with forty beats a minute and I sped it up to 120. I next figured out how to programme the drums and use my other equipment and I wrote my first song two days later. About a year and a half after that *Move Your Body* was released.

After the release of *Move Your Body* DJs started hiring keyboard players, telling them to play keyboards like Marshall Jefferson, so it worked out. They all wanted that piano sound that I had created on their records.

The thing was, up until I bought that QX1, drum machine and keyboard, I had never played an instrument in my life. I was able to do what I did because I listened to Led Zeppelin. I heard the tempo changes and it got me thinking.

Led Zeppelin was one of the bands that I went to see in concert. That was in 1977. Bands came to play concerts at a few different venues in Chicago. There was the Chicago Stadium, the Chicago Amphitheatre and sometimes bands would play at Comiskey Park.

I had tickets for two of the Led Zeppelin concerts. They were playing four nights in Chicago. The first night I went was awesome even though I felt that they were dragging a bit and not playing as fast as they do on the record. The second date Jimmy Page threw up on stage and the rest of the concert got cancelled. But on the way out the venue gives us all these rain checks telling us that the next time Led Zeppelin come to town we can use the rain checks to get into the concert. I kept my rain check and stored it in a safe place back at home. Sometime after news hits that Led Zeppelin are going to return to Chicago and I think, 'Great, I can use my rain check and go and see them.' Boom! John Bonham died before the band was able to return.

John Bonham was the greatest, coolest drummer to walk on this earth. Lots of black people liked John Bonham because they thought he played drums like a black dude. He was an unbelievable drummer. No one could drum like him. He played with his wrists which meant he could do little things which made all the difference. Most rock drummers play with their elbows so that they could play louder. I call the guys elbow drummers and when I see one of these drummers I'm like, 'I'm getting out of here.' But when I see a drummer playing with his wrists I know that guy is going to give dynamics and that's what I want to hear. I'm all for that and that's why I liked drummers like John Bonham.

Another musician that really made an impact on me during my teenage years was Jimmy Page. I mean when you think of those long solos that he did, man! He played the greatest guitar solos ever on those Led Zeppelin records. Peter Frampton was another bad motherfucker, very underrated. Just listen to *Lines On My Face* on the *Frampton Comes Alive* album; he did three epic solos on the same song LIVE.

When it came to vocalists, of course there was Robert Plant. There was also Freddie Mercury and John Anderson from YES. I liked Anderson because I could sing like him. Steven Tyler was another guy I really liked to hear. I liked Bowie too but more of his persona and art form than the sound of his voice. His concepts and imagery was out of this world. Bowie was a fun guy to sit around listening to and to talk about.

I listened to a lot of white rock music but there was some black music that I liked. One of the great black guys that I liked was Isaac Hayes. Another was Lou Rawls, that Lou Rawls live album with *In The Evening When The Sun Goes Down* and *The Girl From Ipanema* on it is oh, man! And Quincy Jones is another guy I listened to a lot.

As I moved through my teenage years my record collection naturally expanded. It wasn't just rock music. Earth Wind and Fire were a band whose records I bought. Slave I liked when they first came out but then they had Mark 'Drac' Hicks who played a killer ass solo on slide. Man, he tore that shit up.

The problem for me with black music was that it either about love or sex or dancing. But I found with rock and pop music there was much more of a varied subject matter and it seemed to me to be a lot more creative.

Around that period of seeing Led Zeppelin in concert I also saw bands like Black Sabbath and Aerosmith, I even went to see the New York Dolls because Leroy talked me into it.

KISS I saw. It's a bit embarrassing but I loved KISS and they had some great songs. I wasn't sure about the make-up thing though. Glam rock kinda passed me by. I didn't really connect with much of that stuff. Thin Lizzy were incredible. Phil Lynott was amazing.

Going to see bands during my teenage years was what I did. I preferred this to going to the sort of things that happened in the high schools. In my first two years at Lindblom because I was a nerd I didn't really have much of a social life. The school would organise dances but I never went to any of those. Another reason why I didn't go was because I couldn't dance. And then by the time I was attending Central Y and hanging out with Bernard. All we did was sit around and get high and listen to music.

It wasn't until my senior year and after I quit my paper round that things started to change, but it didn't mean my social life got any better. I got myself a job bussing dishes. Every weekend I would work at a different restaurant. I got this work because I was signed up with an employment agency and they would contact me when there was an emergency at one of their restaurants and they needed a busboy. A busboy is the guy that takes the dishes off of the table and takes them to the dish washer. He's not the waiter – that is a different job. For some reason they seem to leave the busboys out of those movie scenes.

Bussing dishes meant that I started to get more money coming in than I had when I had been doing my paper round. But what it meant was that because I was working at the weekends I still didn't have much of a social life. If I did get a free weekend and because I had more money in my pocket all I would do is go and hang out with my crew and get everybody high anyway. And those guys are still talking to me about those days. They never had much money so they could only afford like nickel bags of weed, but I would laugh at that and produce an ounce of weed.

CHAPTER TWO
Marshall Jefferson – House Music Pioneer Extraordinaire

I've known Marshall for about thirty years or more. I met Marshall in my senior year at Columbia College Chicago, while multitasking interns at DJ International, Space Place, and Jam Productions, and singing jingles for Proctor and Gardner Advertising Agency, commuting from Gary to Chicago and a single mom. Marshall and I hit it off immediately, he had a quirky/ unique way of making beats and music, not conventional at all. The rhythms were hypnotic and well just made you want to Move Your Body. *We had similar taste in music as well, we both listened to everything, and we knew all kinds of songs from Motown to R&B to Hard Rock to C&W. Midwestern working-class good stock. I trusted him, I still trust and love him. Marshall's the first one to put our form of music into a lyric on a record and add the dance phrase "Jack your Body" Steve Hurley had it to and a few more. However, put them both together. We all added to this collective pool for a new genre complete with name for the genre and a new dance for it as well. So off into the world we went and were still here. Congratulations Marshall J. Jefferson Pioneer and godfather of House Music. Kym Mazelle*

Continuing with my education I went to Western Illinois University to major in accounting. While I was there I hooked up with some new people. In between lessons me, Ed and Kelly (who I think was Steve Silk Hurley's cousin) would hang around the dorm and get stoned.

This was around the 1978 period when punk rock was happening, but that never really touched me, anymore than disco did. I remember when the disco sucks thing went off in Comiskey Park. It was the summer of 79 and there was a game between the Chicago White Sox and the Detroit Tigers. Radio DJ Steve Dahl had organised the Disco Demolition Night; he had a furious anti-disco campaign going on at the time and anticipated a few thousand people to show up to destroy their disco records. Instead an estimated 50,000 showed up and Comiskey Park turned into a bit of a riot zone. Disco wasn't my thing, which I suppose does sound strange, but back in 1979 I might have been one of those people going to destroy disco records too. The problem was disco just got too commercial and this took away the shine of it all. I think that night I probably just stayed home and got stoned, instead.

Being at Western Illinois was fun. I just seemed to spend my days going from room to room getting wasted. I was never a good student but somehow I got through it. The problem was I would go to class and what the teachers said I just seemed to know already. This meant class for me was boring and so I had no motivation. My attitude was, why should I do homework when I know the answers already? I just saw that as a waste of my fuckin' time. There were so many times when the teachers made mistakes and I had to hold myself back from pointing the mistake out and embarrassing them. Instead I just stayed quiet and waited patiently for class to get out and then go and get high.

I was eighteen years old when I started going to Western Illinois University. The drinking laws in Chicago meant you couldn't be served alcohol until you were twenty-one. This meant I didn't hang out in bars. But it didn't mean I couldn't get hold of alcohol and I drank a lot and smoked a lot.

Around this time I also learnt to drive too. The only problem was I couldn't afford a car until a few years later because what money I did earn I spent on buying records and drugs. My friends were always broke too so I would spend money on them too. I got my money by continuing with the busboy jobs. I worked in so many restaurants.

I had a lot of experiences that left an impression on me from this period. One of them found its way onto one of my records called *Mushrooms*. I can't recall how or why but I somehow hooked up with some girls from Florida way. For some reason they'd made their way to Western Illinois. I have no idea why they were even there because they didn't go to the college.

Kelly and me got friendly with these two girls and we'd mess around and hang out together. They told us that they went to school in Florida and that we should go and visit them there. About four months after they went back home Kelly and me went to visit them.

While hooking up with those girls they took us to some field, which I recall was near some big military base. The girls must have been to that field before because they knew exactly what they were looking for. Kelly and me followed them and the next thing we know we are picking mushrooms from the field. We took the mushrooms and it was great. I had my mushroom trip.

The social vibe at Western Illinois was pretty much friendly. It was quite segregated. The black dudes hung out with one another and the white dudes hung out and the two didn't really mix much. Back then there just wasn't much race mixing going on. That's just how it was. People stuck to their comfort zones.

There were few and far opportunities to hang out with white people. I did, but only a few times and this only involved sitting around in some white guy's room listening to rock music and getting high.

I remember listening to a lot of Ted Nugent and Pink Floyd during my college days. It was usually just Kelly, Ed and me listening to this stuff because the other black guys mostly just listened to Rick James and black dance music.

On the few occasions when I did venture out from the dorm it would be to go to a party that one of the fraternities was putting on. It was a popular pastime for the fraternities to throw parties and they could be good fun, even though they weren't really much thing. I really only went to get stoned and meet girls.

I was at college for about three years. In my third year I noticed a huge hiring drive that the post office was doing.

There was a lot of interest for the possibility of a job at the post office and there were long lines of people taking the tests. I took the test and the next thing I knew I was working at the post office.

I did plan to go back to college because this was something my dad wanted me to do. I was thinking about a career in accounting and the average starting salary was only about eleven thousand dollars at that time and I was now working at the post office and getting nearer nineteen thousand dollars, with quarterly raises. So do I go back to school and graduate to make less money, or do I make almost double right now? It was an easy decision.

I worked at the main post office in Chicago which was on 435 West Van Buren. My responsibilities included working the letter sorting machine called a ZMT. I was a ZMT operator with Curtis McClain, who I worked with on songs like *Move Your Body* and *Let's Get Busy*.

To this day I still call Curtis The Dude. Now there's a reason for this. Back in the day when he first started working at the post office he had difficulty remembering people's names. So he was constantly addressing people by saying 'yeah all right dude', 'yeah okay dude', and because of this people turned it around and everybody started calling him The Dude. Damn near forty years later he's still being called The Dude, but that sucker remembers everyone's names now while I can't remember shit!

It was at the post office that I met Curtis. We got on, were the same age and found that we had common interests. We hit it right off the bat from day one. One difference we had at the beginning was that he was into dance music and I was still into my rock.

I would see Curtis at work but we didn't really start hanging out outside of work but what we did start to do was make each other mix tapes. This also started happening around the time that I did start to get into deejaying and into dance music. I sort of had two crews on the go. I had my rock crew with George Byrd and Charles Sanders and a guy called Pony and I had my dance crew that included Curtis, Pop and Brian.

The rock crew would do stupid shit to occupy us and make us laugh and we'd do things like make up holidays. Every day became a holiday with titles like National Kiss the Cat Day. We'd then celebrate these days by going over to Pony's house and getting wasted.

The DJ crew would make mix tapes for each other and we'd play them while we worked. Curtis called himself "Many Mixin Mac" and Pops would call himself radio station WPOP-We Poppin. I didn't have a nickname, damn. Weird because I later came up with such cool group names for my records.

This was the sort of shit I'd do and I liked doing this stuff rather than go to the movies. A lot of the big movies from those days just passed me by. I became a fan of movies in the early 80s after I bought a VCR. It only once I got my VCR that I saw movies like *Blade Runner* and *Star Wars*.

An advantage of working at the post office meant that I was earning enough money to move out of my parents' home and rent an apartment of my own. My place was on the south side of town and it was a pit! Boy it was a pit, but it was my pit and my place. Having my first apartment was exciting and

I could do what I liked and this of course included being able to take women there.

It was a two-bedroom apartment with enough space for me (and the women) but I didn't invite my friends over. No way would I invite my friends over because I knew that they'd fuck up the place. My friends were wild fuckers so no way was I going to let them turn my dive of a home into an even worse dive.

It was around the time of me having my apartment and working at the post office that I met Esther. Esther was my first love, my first proper girlfriend. I met Esther because of her mother, who was also named Esther. Her mother also worked at the post office. I don't know why but for some reason Esther's mother thought I was some kinda gentleman. I suppose I was really. I think Esther's mom had noticed me pursue another postal worker whose name was Regina. Nothing happened with Regina though because she was already engaged. But I would bring her flowers to work and stuff like that and I guess Esther's mom saw this going on.

Esther's mom figured that I should hook up with her daughter and take her to senior prom. I agreed to meet Esther and boom, we hit it off and the next thing you know we're boyfriend and girlfriend.

Esther was a few years younger than me. I think she was eighteen when we went to that prom. Esther was extremely beautiful, an absolute goddess, and she had a great sense of humour. Esther was also extremely smart. She was also extremely clean. I mean clean breath, clean skin. I think she may have been close to an albino, but not sure. Her skin was definitely white but she was African American, if that makes any sense. She liked a lot of alternative music too. She had a wide range in musical taste, just like I did, so this meant we connected musically. We did a lot of out the ordinary stuff together. It was Esther that took me to see the *Rocky Horror Picture Show*; which was fun. Yeah Esther was pretty cool, I would've followed her anywhere.

We stayed together for around five years. It was a very significant relationship for me, but as I got deeper into the music business, that took over and it took me away from her. She also joined the police force and I noticed something in her change and we didn't really connect any more in the ways that we had. We broke up and went our separate ways.

But Esther and me had our fair share of good times. I had my apartment. I was working at the post office and I had money in my pocket. I also started to go out more and party and I went to a place called Nimbus. Nimbus was a south suburban club. What impressed me there was the way the DJ there was able to make a noise that sounded like an aeroplane.

I told Curtis about what I had heard and he explained to me that the DJ did this by phasing in two records together. Curtis described how the DJ was speeding up one record but slowing down the other and that's how he created that incredible sound.

What I had heard in Nimbus inspired and motivated me to go out and buy my own set of decks and a mixer. I wanted to figure out how to make that aeroplane sound and learn to mix. I also had Curtis on hand and everything that I wanted to learn about mixing he already knew.

It was then that I got listening to the Hot Mix 5 because that was the place to learn about how mixing was done. The *Hot Mix 5 Saturday Night Live Ain't No Jive* was a radio show on WBMX which was a black-owned radio station that had been going since 1950.

When the show started in 1981 the host DJs included: Farley 'Jackmaster' Funk, Kenny 'Jammin' Jason, Micky 'Mixing' Oliver, Ralph 'Rockin' Rosario and Scott 'Smokin' Silz. Those guys kept the show going until around 84 when the line-up changed because Silz left and Julian 'Jumpin' Perez joined and then later on he left and Mario 'Smokin' Diaz slipped into his spot. My favorite was Farley and Curtis' favorite was Kenny Jammin Jason.

The show was huge in Chicago; a really big deal for a lot of people. It was popular for a lot of reasons and for me it was the place to hear the best mixing. The DJs were very competitive. They would all play the same songs but they would each mix them in different ways. They would have two copies of every song and this allowed them to do mixing tricks like back spinning, phasing and scratching. They did all kinds of wild and incredible stuff that blew me away. Those guys played something like forty records per hour and on every single song they'd phase, backspin and scratch. It was an amazing thing to hear.

The Hot Mix 5 show started out on a Saturday night but due to its popularity they also did other days and some lunch times too. Each DJ was allocated an hour and would play a very eclectic mix of records. As an example you had Farley playing black disco and then you had Kenny playing white disco. All of the Hot Mix 5 would play European music from the likes of Divine and Kraftwerk. They'd also play the stuff that was coming out New York and Philadelphia too. Those guys would basically play anything that was grooving.

For me each Hot Mix 5 show was like a tutorial in how to do excellent mixing.

What those guys did has been the best mixing I have ever heard. There'd be very few mistakes. I think Farley did but that was because he was the most experimental and he was the most reckless. Farley was the first of the Hot Mix 5 to start scratching and he just went crazy with it. I also think it was Farley who announced that he was going to start playing House music – the music of the future. From that point on everybody just going crazy over House music.

So with the Hot Mix 5 providing me with mixing tutorials and Curtis teaching me too I got busy with my decks. My first decks were Pioneers and a Gemini mixer. In time I discovered that I needed better decks so I went out and bought some decks made by Thorens. Those decks were something else. The sound quality on them was unbelievable and the control you had with them was really good too. My Thorens decks were belt driven and were just fine for a time but I had to get even better so I bought some Technics and, once I had those, I could do all the stuff like back spinning and get closer to what the Hot Mix 5 were able to do.

I kept the decks set up in my apartment and spent hours messing around on them. The only time I took them out was when I was going to play at a party or something.

The first time I played out as a DJ was at a place called Studio 21 which was on 95th Street. It was me and my friend Bernard Howard who threw the party. My set that night included songs like *The Music's Got Me* by Visual and *Let's Go Dancing* by Sparque; both really good tracks to dance to. I also played tracks that night like *Can You Move* by Modern Romance and *In the Name Of Love* by the Thompson Twins. That was the kinda stuff that was getting played around 83/84 when we put that party on.

Even though I was playing those sorts of records out I still loved my rock music. No way was I going to shelve rock music. It still had a place in my life and in my record collection. As a matter of fact I upgraded my sound system in my apartment which meant I could enjoy my rock music even more because I could hear it played a lot louder.

It was around the time of upgrading my home sound system and getting deeper into becoming a DJ that I started to also build my own speakers. I built some huge speakers that I could take out and DJ with. I didn't even know if I could actually build the damn things but I went out and got an electric saw and some wood and all the parts that I would need and the next thing I know there are these huge speaker cabinets in my apartment. I had an amplifier too that had 1500 watts and that was loud.

I now had my decks and my speakers and my amplifier and my record collection was growing by the day. But I couldn't do that many parties because of my job at the post office and around that time I was on the graveyard shift; which meant that I worked through the night – midnight until eight thirty. And because that was the prime party time, I missed out on deejaying publicly. As a temporary solution, I started promoting a DJ named Steve Zinnemon. Steve was awesome and I figured that I could put up the money for the parties and he could spin while I was at the post office.

The first party was at a place called the Crystal Palace, where the House DJ was a guy named Tony Bowie, who went on to make records on Mitchball. Tony literally lived at the Crystal Palace. Tony was eventually joined by Jimi Polo, who made hits like *Better Days* and *Shake Your Body*. Jimi didn't live there but he was over there a lot.

I bought a bunch of Steve Zinnemon posters and put them up all over the city. I only found out years later about the promotion wars that were going on. All my posters got torn down and replaced with other parties within hours. That meant that when the Crystal Palace party finally went down, it was completely empty. I got there the next day and my speakers were gone. I called up Steve and he tells me he has them and he's not giving them back, then he hangs up on me. I keep calling and his sister picks up. I tell her I need my speakers and she tells me I'm not getting them. I then say I'm calling the cops and she tells me if I do, I'd better watch my back.

Now I guess if this turns into a movie Hollywood would have me going over there and kicking everyone's ass, but what actually happened was I just moved on. Later for them. I got some small measure of satisfaction decades later when Steve contacted me on Facebook asking for help getting into the music business. I wonder if he really thought I'd forgotten. I bought other, better speakers but those I'd built with my own hands. I politely told him I'd look into it and haven't communicated with him since.

A few weeks after that debacle Phil Lambert called me up asking for a ride to Guitar Center. We got there and looked around a little bit before a salesman approached us wanting to show us a new piece of gear-The Yamaha QX-1. Things were about to change big time. You fucked up Steve.

Now that I started to write my own music I started hooking up with Curtis McClain and this was because I had heard him singing while he was at work. Curtis was singing all the time. He sang tunes we all knew but Curtis, having Curtis's sense of humour, would replace some of the lyrics with his own and those would often be obscene substitutes like 'I'll never be your beast of burden my dick is hard and my balls are hurting'. But Curtis had a voice, he could sing and there was never going to be any debate about him not being the singer on my songs.

Curtis was lively – one of the liveliest! A real live wire! He was useful to have around too because he actually had some musical knowledge. He played drums but he put them to one side and switched to learning how to play guitar and I have heard people say that he was a really good guitar player. But once he started deejaying and he stopped playing guitar. And then once he started singing he stopped deejaying, too.

Once Curtis started getting into making music he didn't want to be known as a DJ. For some reason he didn't even want people to know that he had been a DJ. Even to this day I tell him that he should start being a DJ again and get out there and play House music to people. He was a brilliant DJ. He really knew his stuff but he'd say 'No, man, I'm no DJ I'm a singer man'. I don't know why he felt that way, but that's the way he was.

The music side of things really started to heat up and another significant event was my visit to a club in Chicago called the Music Box. There was a girl I knew called Veronica Montgomery, but she told everyone to call her Lynn. Now she had a B.O.D.Y., phew! She had curves to talk about. We became friends and we'd hang out together. She had a strange way of dressing. It was slightly Goth, but not all the way. But what she did wear was very curve-flattering.

I saw her dressed one day in some very tight clothing and could tell that she was heading out some place, so I asked her where she was going and she told me that she was going to the Music Box. She invited me to go with her, so I did and as soon as I walked into the club the sound hit me. Up until that point that club had the loudest sound system that I had ever heard in my life. I mean the bass would physically move your body. Boom, boom, boom and you feel the vibrations pushing you. Damn, it was so fuckin' loud man.

It was pitch black inside the Music Box. There was only one light bulb and that was very dim. You literally could not see anything inside the club. There were no chairs and no tables. All you had was the dance floor and that was all the people needed.

There was no telling what was going on, on that dance floor, because it was so dark. Lynn tried pulling me onto the dance floor a few times but I resisted because I wasn't a dancer. Plus no way was I cheating on Esther.

You had the area where the DJ was positioned and that was Ron Hardy. He was elevated and looked down onto the crowd on the dance floor. Ron Hardy was something else. He had that place going wild. He'd do stuff like take out the bass and just leave the treble and he'd keep that going and then he'd bring everything back in with a boom!

That first night I went to the Music Box I just got so into the music that Ron was playing and the vibe that he created in the club. I was into the Hot Mix 5 vibe but was I was hearing was underground. In fact what was going on in the Music Box was under the underground.

Ron would play great records and a real mixture. The first song that I heard him play at the Music Box was *Let No Man Put Asunder* by First Choice. It was the Frankie Knuckles mix. The next record he played was *The Look of Love* by ABC. Then he played *Hip Hop Be Bop* by Man Parrish. All of these songs were completely different but running through them all was that incredibly loud and powerful bass.

There were a lot of gay people that went to the Music Box. There were a lot of straight people too, but around that time when I first went it was mostly all gay people. The club started out as a gay club but once it got more popular, that changed.

The history of the Music Box had started after a guy called Robert Williams started to use Ron following the departure of another DJ he had been using called Frankie Knuckles. Williams had set up the Warehouse Club in Chicago and he'd brought Frankie Knuckles in from New York to Chicago. But Frankie left to start up his own club called the Power Plant.

Ron had been a Chicago DJ since 1974 and his club was Den One. He'd then left Chicago for a while and had gone out to Los Angeles. But once he returned he became the Music Box DJ. This was in 1982.

When I first started going to the Music Box I had no idea who Ron Hardy was. At when I went to the Music Box he was just another DJ to me. It was as I got more into being a DJ and spending at least 200 dollars a week on records that I started to get to know Ron.

In those days 200 dollars was a lot of money. I bought a lot of my records from a guy called Chip E. Chip E worked at a record store called Importes Etc. The store had been opened by a guy called Paul Weisberg in 1981. He'd been a DJ himself since the late 70s. The store was about ten people wide and quite long and there were some stairs positioned at one end. The location of the store was in a garage in a side street in Printers Row which is in an area known as the Loop in South Chicago. Traditionally the area had a lot of printing and publishing businesses located there.

Now this independent record shop was the first to include a section called 'Warehouse Music' and it's said that Chip E was the first to shorten warehouse to just 'house' to describe the music that was becoming popular in Chicago.

I also bought a lot of records from another guy called Jesse Jones who was from Master C & J, who had the House track *When You Hold Me*, worked in the other popular Chicago record store called Loop Records.

Guys like Chip E and Jesse Jones recognised me as a DJ but at the time of going to the Music Box Ron didn't know of me at all. I did get to know him. I'd listen to his set and be in awe at the way he mixed. I mean his mixing was pretty spot on. Sadly as time went on it got sloppier as a result of his drug habit taking over.

There was times when Ron's heroin use made me angry. There was times when I drove him to places to get it. I didn't know that was what he was needing my ride for and after I found out I was supremely pissed off. For all I knew when he asked me to take him to an address I just thought I was helping the guy out. I didn't know I was helping him to get his fucking drugs, man.

I remember there was this one time when I took Ron and a guy called Harry Dennis from Jungle Wonz to get what I discovered was their drugs and I was really pissed with them and told them straight that was the last time I would give them a lift anywhere. I told them to never come to me with that bullshit again.

I do recall the first time I ever had contact with Ron at the Music Box. It was soon after I had done *I've Lost Control* with Sleezy D. I had a recording of the track on cassette. This was what we did back then. We'd make the song and record it onto a cassette and take it to the various DJs at the clubs. I took a cassette with *I've Lost Control* on it and handed it to Ron in the Music Box and then I just walked away. As I said, it was so dark in the place Ron probably didn't even see who had given him the cassette. That track included me doing the screaming noise and it was Sleezy saying the words 'I've lost control'. It all happened very spontaneously and was done right there on the spot. I already had the music made and when

Sleezy came down to my basement he started dancing to it and that was when I said to him, 'Hey man, you wanna do some vocals on this?' He said yeah and got all fired up and that was when we recorded him saying 'I've lost control' and I pitched in with the screams. I think we captured the vibe of someone losing control.

So Ron now had the cassette with *I've Lost Control* on it and I then just enjoyed the rest of the night in the club and left. I was still at the post office at this time and I was still doing my graveyard shift; which for a period around that time changed so that I had to work on Tuesday and Saturday nights. These were the two nights that the Music Box opened, so this meant that for about five months I didn't go there.

All the time that I wasn't going to the Music Box Sleezy D was and he'd been telling me about the vibe and how Ron was 'jacking the cut' at the Music Box. Sleezy was really excited about this and I thought great and handed him another cassette with another five or six of my songs on it and I told him to give it to Ron.

I didn't know to what extent Ron was playing my stuff in the club. At best I imagined he'd play a song once or maybe even twice throughout the entire night. But what I learned was that each of my songs had become like anthems in the Music Box and was getting played over and over throughout the night.

Once I found this out I realised that I needed to get back to the Music Box and find out for myself what sort of reception my songs were getting. And so after about six months I finally get back down to the club. On the night I went with Sleezy and as we approach the club all the doormen are like 'Sleezy, Sleezy, it's Sleezy! Hey, go right in man'. So Sleezy just walks right in and I get stopped at the door by those guys. Of course, they had no idea who I was. Sleezy had to tell the doormen that I was with him and I then got let in. What I didn't realise was that the doormen and lots of other people in the club thought it was Sleezy who had made all those songs on that cassette that Ron was playing in the club.

That night Ron played all of my songs just like Sleezy had told me and hearing my songs on that loud Music Box sound system was just something else. I could never have imagined how amazing my songs could have sounded being played that loud and with so much bass. It was really exciting.

So I started to connect with Ron. In appearance he was an average size guy around 5'9". He had an average build too. He wasn't overweight and he wasn't skinny. He could be good company.

For a time Ron started to live in the Music Box and actually had his bed positioned in the DJ box. I was often going down there. I'd bang on the back door and Ron would let me in and we'd hang out and play the cassettes with my latest music on it. I was very interested to hear what Ron thought about my songs because he knew what would work for the people that came to the Music Box.

I remember there'd be times when one of my cassettes would be playing and Ron and I would be talking and, while we were doing that, Ron would pause the cassette tapes while he was rolling a joint or cigarette laced with heroin. It was as if Ron's mind could work on twenty different things at one time. That was Ron Hardy; he could be off in so many directions while being in one spot.

Ron had a lot of confidence and even arrogance when he was in that DJ box. He would do things like call the crowd in the club his children. Even when we'd be listening to my cassettes in his DJ box-come-bedroom he'd say stuff like 'Yeah man, my children will love this track'.

To the people that went to the Music Box Ron Hardy was God. People loved him. There were so many times when I saw and heard people praise Ron. There was one time when I saw this guy go up to the DJ box and shout out 'Hey Ron can you make me a tape?' and Ron replies back 'Sure, I'll make you a tape, give me twenty dollars'. The man returned with 'Twenty dollars?' and Ron shouts back 'Man, it's worth forty dollars'.

I heard that once the heroin took over and Ron was struggling with his addiction, he did make tapes to sell to people and he also sold off his records, just so that he could get the money to pay for his heroin. I didn't get to see this side of Ron because I was heavily involved with my music career by then and away travelling and stuff. I honestly think that Ron wouldn't have wanted me to see that side of him and what he became. I think he would have been embarrassed. I'm also glad that I didn't see that desperate side of Ron. I'm able to remember Ron Hardy as a great DJ, the best, and as a friend who loved my music and helped get me my break in the music industry.

Ron Hardy will be remembered for many things and his contribution to the beginnings of Chicago House music has been recognised and applauded. He also left us a track called

Sensation. This was issued on Trax Records in 1985. It was co-written with Vince Lawrence and supposedly produced by Larry Sherman. Actually I kinda didn't like the record. From what I know Vince heard a track that Ron was playing in the Music Box and decided to take into Universal Studios; which was the biggest recording studios in town at that time. Some of the greats had recorded there: Nat King Cole, Frank Sinatra, Buddy Rich, Duke Ellington. It was the go-to spot in Chicago.

There was a guy called Richard Fairbanks, he was Screamin' Rachael's boyfriend at the time and a sound engineer involved with Universal Studios. Larry cut some deal with Richard that included putting Trax stuff out like Screamin' Rachael's *My Main Man*.

Sensation went into the studio and the guys recorded a really cleaned up version. But by doing so I think the song lost a lot of the edge it had originally had and it no longer sounded like it had in the Music Box. But *Sensation* got released and Ron Hardy put his name on it.

I think Duane Grant played keyboards on *Sensation* and Adrienne Jett sang the vocals. Her name was spelt wrongly on the record. Adrienne also sang some vocals on Jamie Principles' *Your Love*.

Later I worked on a song that I was calling *The Pleasure Exchange*. That song ended up being called *Under You* and the first recordings had vocals on it; which Adrienne Jett sang on, but I had to remove from the recordings because I couldn't afford to pay her. Larry Sherman stepped in and agreed to pay her if I allowed him to release the song as a Trax Records song.

CHAPTER THREE

So, I have been asked to say a little bit about my man Marshall Jefferson and the Sleeze is honoured to do so. Me and MJ go way back and in the House community I may have the longest friendship with him. We met before either of us even thought about making records or deejaying. I'm talking late 70s. What we had was love of clubbing and getting it in. Marshall's first nickname for our crew was 'The Fun Guys' and that we were. In the 80s MJ had a regular job (yes hard to believe yet true). I remember the day Marshall gave me a call and told me that he had just bought some equipment and we were gonna make music. I came straight over after coming from the Power Plant (Frankie's spot that changed my life forever) and we just started playing with beats and sounds and I have no shame in saying I was 'in it' to say the least. That first day and night it was obvious that MJ had a feel for it. Me, I love to dance so coming up with beats and things I could do, but Marshall, he was finding new sounds, patterns and as fast I could try to describe a vibe, he was making it happen. He made I've Lost Control *in his basement, went with what we felt and took a reel down to Ron Hardy at the 'Underground' on Lower Wacker Drive (one of the other spots that helped shape the Sleeze) and*

from the crowd's reaction, well, let's just say that some now call it the first acid track and it was the first one we released. Marshall has never looked back and over thirty years later is a House music legend and icon and that's the facts. I often say 'it ain't easy being Sleezy' but have to give credit where due as far as the music, it wouldn't be a Sleezy D without a Marshall J.
Sleezy D

Another important club that ran alongside the Music Box was the Power Plant. The Power Plant was Frankie Knuckle's club, which ran between 1982 and 1987.

The first time I went to the Power Plant I got locked in the club with all the other clubbers and the guys running the place didn't let us out until two o'clock that afternoon. Apparently for some reason on that night Frankie told the guys he worked with at the club to lock the doors saying 'I'm about to get off'. The guys protested, reminding Frankie that there was fire laws but Frankie was like 'Lock the motherfucking doors, I'm about to get off' and so the doors were locked and nobody could get out. The doors were actually chained and so there I was, with all these other people locked in the Power Plant and Frankie Knuckles got off.

Frankie was a couple of years older than me. He was from New York and had grown up in the Bronx. He became friends with Larry Levan, the DJ at the legendary Paradise Garage and the two of them deejayed together at places like The Gallery and the Continental Baths. Back then they played soul and disco. It was sometime in the late seventies that Frankie left

New York and came to Chicago where he joined Robert Williams at The Warehouse.

I remember Robert William's telling me that towards the end of the Warehouse Frankie didn't like the direction that the club had gone in. I was told that he seemed to have something against the amount of straight people that had started to turn up at the club; which had been mostly a gay club. I don't why Frankie felt that way.

The Warehouse crowd did change from what it started out as. My cousin Adrienne and her art student friends used to go there. When we'd have family gatherings, Adrienne would bring along some of the music that she'd heard Frankie play at the Warehouse and my cousin Johnny would tease her, calling it that old "house" music, meaning gay music that they played at the Warehouse.

Adrienne loved the Warehouse and she was known as one of the people that would close down the club. That meant that she'd be there until the very end. I recall her telling me that after the Warehouse she and her friends would be so hyped up that they'd then go to the movies just to try and wind down.

In 2010 Adrienne came with me when I was shooting a video and Robert also showed up. As soon as he saw her he remembered her and said, 'You, you used to close down the Warehouse' and they had a good laugh about those Warehouse days.

Robert Williams was another good guy. He was from New York and he also contributed to the birth and development of House music. He should get the credit he deserves for bringing together a lot of people in the clubs that he opened.

I think Robert tried to get Larry Levan to Chicago before he got Frankie but Larry was like 'I ain't going to no Chicago'. So Larry stayed in New York and Chicago got Frankie and the Warehouse took off. I think Frankie's attitude was that he could come to Chicago and be a big fish in a small pond.

I worked with Frankie. I felt that our sessions were what could be described as instructional. What I mean by that is that when we were in the studio together I had to show him various things about how something worked. When I first went into the studio with him I felt very intimidated. I kind of took for granted that Frankie knew his way around the studio because he was Frankie Knuckles – one of the biggest DJs in town.

The first time I actually met Frankie was in the studio. Some of his people called up my people and a meeting was set up because Frankie wanted to remix some of my songs. At the time it was to do some mixes for *Move Your Body* and this was before the song had even been released. What Frankie done was great but it wasn't anything special and so those mixes never got released.

Frankie also did a remix of my song called *Ride the Rhythm*. Kevin Irving also did a version of that song. Mickey Oliver did the mix on Kevin's version. I did two versions of that song. One included vocals from Kevin and the other from Curtis McClain. It was some time after Kevin's version that I did my version and, at that time, I wasn't even aware that Kevin had done a recording of my song. At first Kevin thought I had ripped him off and we had to have a meet-up to discuss it.

Frankie spoke in a very even-toned manner. He never seemed to get excited or show excitement. There was only one time that I did see him get excited. At the time we were in the studio and it was the first time that he heard Byron Stingily singing. But once he had that moment of getting excited he quickly reeled it in. It was as if he didn't want other people to see him get excited.

Over the years I would mostly only see Frankie as he was coming out of the DJ box and I was about to go in. I wasn't ever one for going to the after parties at these places. I much preferred to just head back to the hotel. The thing is most of the music business happens at those after parties. I think this happens across the whole entertainment business: music, acting, theatre. But I would avoid those damn after parties like the plague, especially since I stopped getting high back in the 80s. So not going to those parties meant I missed on properly catching up with guys like Frankie. But there was this one time when we did manage to hang out and talk at length. It was around the early 90s and I was thinking of quitting the music industry. It was Frankie who talked me into sticking with it. He convinced me that I still had so much to give to the music business and to House music. There was even some talk about hooking me up with the Def mix team, that included Frankie and David Morales and Satoshi Tomiie and Judy Weinstein but that was never going to happen because I knew that Judy Weinstein, his manager, still hated my guts from an incident in the 80s, which I'll get to later.

Frankie and me stayed friends right up until he died in 2014. We actually saw each other three months before he passed on because we were both billed to play at a club in Manchester on New Year's Eve. We saw each other and we gave each other a hug and had a chat about what we'd both been up to. Of course I didn't know that would be the last time that I would see him. Frankie died as a result of some complications relating to the Type II diabetes that he'd been living with for quite a few years.

My philosophy on House music comes because of Frankie Knuckles and what he played in the Warehouse. Frankie basically played the best underground House music and throughout my whole career my philosophy has always been to ask myself, Would Frankie have played this at the Warehouse? The song could be any style: disco, Italo dance, European electro music or it could be Detroit techno, but if it's cool and its underground Frankie would have played it at the Warehouse. When I first did *Move Your Body* everybody said it wasn't House music because it had that piano on it and at that stage nobody had made a House record that used piano all over it. But Frankie Knuckles and Ron Hardy both played it and, for me, that meant it was a House record.

There was another song too that Byron and I worked together on called *I Can't Stay Away* by Ragtyme. Byron and I produced we recorded it in Chicago Tracks Recording Studios – which is a different thing to Trax Records. This song was released in 1987 on Bright Star Records and featured Byron Stingily on vocals. We got Frankie Knuckles, Ron Hardy, and Lil Louis all to mix it – in the same studio session. I'd given them all the demo and they all loved it and asked to mix it.

What I remember from that *I Can't Stay Away* session was Ron's crew and Frankie's crew ganging up on Lil Louis. For some reason they looked down on him and would mess him around. Some of this may have been because he came from the West Side of Chicago and that was a pretty rough part of town. At that time Frankie and Ron lived on the north side, and most of the people from that part of town looked down on west-side people.

Lil Louis hit the limelight with *French Kiss*. I thought the song was a pretty nice dance song. I liked the crescendo and the way it built and built before slowing right down before speeding back up again. At the time of its release I don't think anyone imagined it would get as big as it got. It was a huge hit.

So you had all these DJs making names for themselves and back in the 70s and 80s a club would only have one DJ. There'd be one DJ and that would be their club. Guys like Frankie or Ron Hardy would play for like twelve hours straight. A club was the DJ's home. Back then there was no such thing as guest DJs. There was one club and one DJ and it was that DJ that made that particular club. That was why the Music Box was known as being Ron Hardy's club and the Warehouse was known as being Frankie Knuckles' club. Both were legendary clubs with legendary DJs.

Another thing about those clubs like the Warehouse and the Music Box was that they were alcohol-free zones. Those places didn't have licences to sell alcohol and that's not what the people wanted or needed anyway.

There'd be a lot of water available and sometimes there'd be punch too. I've heard some people say that there was acid in the punch, but I drank plenty of that punch and I never got high on it. Maybe somebody did lace the punch with acid a couple of times but it wasn't a week in, week out thing. No way!

The kids had their own drugs anyway and they'd just take their own drugs into the clubs. The popular drugs being used around that time was MDMA.

Methylenedioxymethamphetamine better known as MDMA at the time was being used all over the States throughout the 70s and 80s. People in Chicago had been using it since 1970. It was only in the mid 80s that the government banned it and it was around that mid 80s period that people in the UK started to get hold of it.

I took MDMA too but I calmed down a lot once I was getting work in the music industry. But the main drugs going around were weed, MDMA, some coke and some heroin. Coke was found more in the commercial clubs and MDMA was found more in the underground clubs like the Music Box and the Warehouse.

Another Chicago club that has its place in House music history was Den One. This club was even before the Warehouse. That was Ron Hardy's club before the Music Box. Den One was before the Warehouse too but was a much smaller club. So Chicago had Den One, the Warehouse and then the Music Box and the Power Plant running at the same time. There were other key people in Chicago too that helped popularize House music.

Ron Hardy taught a guy called Wayne Williams how to DJ. It was Wayne who sang the vocals on the House track

Undercover by Dr Derelict. This track was released by Jesse Saunders on his Jes Say Record label in 1984. He also produced it. Wayne went on to become the A&R man for R Kelly and also organise the Chosen Few Picnic and Festival that still runs to this day in Chicago. Wayne had been responsible for setting up the Chosen Few Dance Corp back in the late 70s and that had included Jesse Saunders, Alan King and Tony and Andre Hachett. All of those guys really helped to take House music to the masses.

The Mendel High School also needs to be mentioned because that was also a significant place in the history of House in Chicago. Mendel was a Catholic school that had been opened in the early 50s.

There were parties being held at Mendel where the music being played was what we called European and alternative. The reason this music got played was a deliberate attempt to keep the gangsters away.

Some parties were called punk outs and gangsters didn't want to be seen at a party where that was the name. It worked too because the gangsters stayed away from those parties and left people like me and my friends alone.

The reason we didn't want gangsters at our punk outs was because the gangsters carried guns. We didn't want guns at our parties, we just wanted to listen to music and dance. The gangsters couldn't stand our music. They liked funk man. For them it was all about Funkadelic, Parliament and James Brown. That was stepping music. That was mid-tempo stuff. But Mendel wasn't having any of that stuff. Mendel was playing much faster music, European, disco, New York. I think some of the members of the Chosen Few played at Mendel, but I'm not sure.

Mendel parties really blew up and a lot of those kids went onto become the people who went to the Music Box and the Power Plant. Some just grew older and moved on to do other things.

Sauers was another popular venue. That was a place that Farley played at. He also played at the Playground and First Impressions. These were all very commercial clubs compared to places like the Music Box and the Power Plant. Places like Sauers were much better lit and they actually had furniture in them. But they were still like a poor man's disco really and they didn't serve alcohol, either.

Sauers and the Playground were located in mid-town Chicago. This area was right next to the projects but people from the projects didn't have much to do with the clubs because the DJs played House music.

Farley was a character. He was one of those unforgettable guys. I still meet people to this day who say 'Oh man, you play House music do you? I met this guy twenty-five years ago' and they go on to tell me about the time they met Farley. Once you meet Farley you never forget him.

Back in the day Farley would enter the room and he'd have everybody sweating. We were all scared of Farley, man. He could be very intimidating and he could really embarrass you. The thing with Farley was that he had no filter. He'd just say whatever came into his head.

CHAPTER FOUR

I still play Move Your Body *in my sets today, and the crowd always goes totally wild. This track is timeless and it uplifts the soul. Just like all of Marshall's music he sets the standard for quality and integrity and, he will live forever through his sounds.*
Smokin' Jo

It was after my first night of going to the Music Box that I started to move towards making music. But that still didn't happen for a few months. In fact a lot of things happened for me in a very short space of time.

With the sound of that big ass Music Box sound system still ringing in my ears I moved back home to live with my parents again. I just needed to chill for a little while. I wasn't really into keeping up a home all by myself either. I set up my decks and equipment and my huge speakers in the basement and I would blast out my music.

Around this time Jesse Saunders came out with *On And On* but I hadn't actually started to make any music of my own at this point. I was happy just being a DJ. One day I was in Loop Records. I looked up and noticed a sign saying 'Jesse

Saunders Hot Hot Hot'. The twelve-inch of his record had just come out. I bought two copies, something I did all the time back then. I took the record home and played it and the first thing that hit me was how primitive the record sounded. I thought it was raw and the worst produced song that I had ever heard in my life. I was like, what the fuck? As I listened to that record and something went off inside my head and I thought 'Man! I can do better than this'. It was after this that I went to the music store and I bought all that equipment that I needed to make my own songs.

By the time *On And On* came out Jesse Saunders was already an established and popular DJ in Chicago and people called his record House. Jesse was the king in the beginning. He made some money from selling records in the early days and he stood out. Just as House music started to take off Jesse was the pride of DJs in Chicago. He was the first one of us to actually start to make some money from making House music and in many ways he was the template for the high-paid DJ. Once guys like me saw what Jesse was achieving he became the goal for us to aim for too. We all wanted to be like Jesse and have what Jesse had.

The reason he had to put *On And On* out on Jes Say Records was because he was in Chicago and the big record companies weren't interested in us and what House music was. I mean *On And On*, there was no way a song like that was going to get picked up by one of the majors.

There was a guy around Chicago known as Leonard Remix Roy. He wrote a book and in that book he says that he was the first person to use the term House. He was a DJ too but I don't think he had a connection to the Warehouse club and so he didn't know that people started to call a certain sound of music House. But Farley has admitted that he got the name from Leonard and blew it up over the radio.

After *On And On* and the frequent use of the term House and Farley announcing on the radio that he was playing House music – the music of the future, House music started to take off like wildfire.

I was aware of House music blowing up and I wanted to be part of it and, to be honest, I don't really know who really came up with the term House music. I just know that it was associated with Frankie Knuckles' Warehouse club and it referred to a specific sort of music. At the time House didn't refer to a sort of genre, it referred to the music that people like Ron and Frankie played.

On And On was the first House record. The significance of *On And On* is that it got so many people getting into making music, myself among them. Until Jesse came along with *On And On* nobody thought they could make a song. If Jesse hadn't come along and made *On And On* I would still be working at the post office. If Jesse hadn't made *On And On* House music would never have left Chicago. Chicago would have ended up like Atlanta where they are a load of brilliant DJs but none of them ever made a record. And because nobody made a record, nobody left the city.

On And On came out on Jes Say Records. This was Jesse Saunders's own label. It was Vince Lawrence who designed the logo for the label. He wrote Jes Say in his own hand. *Undercover* by Dr Derelict was the second House record. This was also Jesse Saunders and Vince Lawrence with Wayne Williams and it was also released on Jes Say Records. I actually liked that record more than *On And On* because I felt there was some progression. It also had singing on it which I liked. I was immediately with the programme and I went out and bought two copies of that, too.

It was Vince Lawrence who produced my first record. My first record was *Virgo Go Wild Rhythm Trax*. I released that record on my own label which I called Other Side Records. I took a page out of Vince's book and I wrote all the labels up in my own hand. My record came about after I read the notes on Jesse's record. It said Precision Record Labs and it had the address which was 38th Western and 32nd Street and I went down there. That was where I met Vince. Vince was the visionary for Chicago House music. His father had owned some pissant record label so he'd been around making music and he saw something in House music and what was possible.

When I first took my songs to Vince he listened but kinda said 'That part won't work and that part won't work either' and I was kinda knocked back. I mean I thought making a record in a studio was going to be much easier. But what I discovered was that making a record in a studio with Vince was an extremely difficult thing to do. Nowadays it's a whole different ball game and if I had to do my first record again I could knock that out in say an hour. The *Virgo Go Wild Rhythm Trax* sessions took about two weeks to do. And that was just to do eight fucking drum tracks.

When I first met Vince I had the impression that I was dealing with a hustler. He seemed to be the type that chased money and wanted to get paid. He talked fast and you really had to be able to keep up with him. Vince also came across as someone who was very sure of himself and convinced you that he knew everything about being in the studio, so you were always left thinking 'Wow, this man knows everything'. Vince was a fun guy. He was good to be around.

In those days Vince was down the studio twenty-four hours a day. He was pressing up the records for Larry Sherman. I got talking to Vince and he told me how I could get my record pressed up there. I had money in my pocket and I had made some songs and I was ready to go and have a record pressed. It cost me fifteen hundred dollars to have a thousand copies pressed up. That was a pretty straight forward deal and Larry told me that after that it would cost less money to have more records pressed. The next thing I know Larry's also talked me into allowing him to distribute my record for me too. I actually hand wrote the titles of the songs onto those records.

My *Virgo* record started to get played on the radio and the DJs around Chicago were playing it. This was okay but I didn't get too excited about it. I remember the Hot Mix 5 playing it but I knew I had stronger songs in the pipeline. A part of me just saw the *Virgo* record as a bunch of drum tracks and they were but they hadn't been like that at first and I had other stuff with music on them and I wanted the world to hear them. I felt like I had pricked people with a little pin but what I had in coat pocket was a .44 Magnum and I was going to blow their heads off with my other songs.

I would hear those *Virgo* songs being played in the clubs but I honestly didn't feel too proud about it. Of course Sleezy

D thought it was amazing and he got really excited about it. But it was my first release and that was something.

The reason I used the name *Virgo* was simple. I'm a Virgo, an earth sign. After my record came out everybody started calling me Virgo and that stuck for a while. But I got kinda disillusioned about making records. After that studio experience with Vince I just thought it was too difficult and I disappeared for a few months.

During that time I didn't make any more music and nobody really saw me around much. Vince and Larry must have thought the same too. I guess they just figured I had gotten out of the music business.

Trusting Larry with the distribution of my record turned out to be a big mistake and in time a lot of other Trax Record artists would also discover the same too. Royalties, what were royalties?

But after those months of being out of the way I re-emerged. I went down to the Music Box and Ron was playing a bunch of my songs and people were going wild over them. He played *I've Lost Control* like five times that night and I started thinking 'Wow, I'm the man' again. And so after that night I got back into making music again.

Now while I hadn't been around Vince had made *Virgo Tracks Again* and this had been released as a twelve-inch on Trax Records. I didn't feel too great about that and it felt to me like Trax was just trying to cash in on my name and the success of *Virgo Go Wild Rhythm Trax*.

I figured that *Virgo Go Wild Rhythm Trax* must have done something and sold enough records for Trax to want to use the

Virgo name. I just thought, well if that piece of shit can do all right then what I have next is going to be much better.

What happened next was that I met Adonis. He was a friend of a guy called Rudy Forbes who I knew from the post office. Rudy brought Adonis over to my place to listen to some of my music. At that time he wasn't known as Adonis though as he was calling himself Mighty Mike.

The first thing I noticed about Adonis was that he talked really fast. Around that time he also seemed to kiss ass a lot too. He played bass and that was partly why Rudy had brought him to me. The idea was that he might be able to put on bass onto my music. He didn't actually end up playing any bass on any of my songs though.

Adonis did have some equipment of his own. Among his collection was a TB303 and unlike a lot of us he actually knew how to work the thing. It was on that TB303 that I first heard the bassline that was on *No Way Back*. When I heard it I said 'Man that's a jamming fucking bassline, let's work on that'. But he was like no way man, that's mine. What we did do though was an EP and *No Way Back* was supposed to be one of the songs on it.

In the end the four songs that found their way onto the EP was *Free Yourself, Under You, R U Hot Enough* and *My Space*. *My Space* was a track by Adonis and me. Adonis played the bassline on that song. The EP was released by Trax under my name, Virgo.

R U Hot Enough was the song that replaced *No Way Back*. Adonis released *No Way Back* on Trax and he followed this up with a massive hit called *We're Rockin' Down the House* and, he became a House master.

I remember going to one of Farley's parties and during the night he throws Adonis' *No Way Back*. Now coincidentally Larry Sherman was also at that party and he saw the reaction that the kids gave those songs and wanted it. But I think Adonis must have spoken to Larry because when I talked to Adonis about the Larry wanting the songs for the EP he said 'No fuck that man, I'm going to put *No Way Back* out on its own and it's going to be on Trax Records'.

Trax Records now had my *I've Lost Control*, the *Virgo Go Wild Rhythm Trax* and the EP. Out of all of those releases Adonis had the biggest hit with *No Way Back*. That's just the way that worked out at that time. After *No Way Back* and the EP came out Adonis and I stayed in touch and we did still hang out.

Even with all this stuff coming out on Trax Records I still wasn't signing any contracts with the label. Not many people did but there was a few. I saw people sign contracts and on occasion I even tried to talk someone out of signing a contract. One time Sleezy and I sat in the car outside Trax Records with two guys for three hours trying to persuade them not to sign a contract. In the end they did sign it because they just wanted their record out.

Trax Records was Larry Sherman, Vince Lawrence and Jesse Saunders. Their label was formed in 1984 and they issued their first record called *Wanna Dance* by Le Noiz. Le Noiz was Jesse Saunders.

Larry had an assistant whose name was Sandy. At first I thought she was Larry's wife but it turned out that they weren't married at all. She was short and wore coke bottle glasses.

Trax was located in one big room with an office and a lathe in it. There were a handful of chairs. In a room down stairs there was the record-pressing machine and loads of boxes of records piled up everywhere.

Trax Records would be the leading House music record label for many years and during its time put several releases out from myself, Frankie Knuckles, Phuture, Kevin Irving, Mr Fingers and many others. Trax really did help to introduce House music to the world outside of Chicago.

CHAPTER FIVE

Marshall's music is the very essence of what House Music is all about. A pillar of strength for the very foundations of the ground on which our House was built.
Mr C

I suppose the post office can take some credit for *Move Your Body*. It was while I was working one of the graveyard shift that I heard the tune in my head. In those night-time hours I would hear songs drift into my mind as I was falling asleep on the job. I would be there working on the ZMT machine and it was all pretty repetitive. It was a mail-sorting machine where sixty letters would come through in sixty seconds. 60659 was the zone in Chicago that Curtis McClain and I worked the machine for. Our section would call ourselves the 59s.

Being a ZMT operator became second nature to Curtis and me. I mean that's what happens when you do the same job night after night. And some nights when things got a little quiet I would daydream about music. I was already making music and I had a lot of ideas going around my head. Once my nightshift had finished I would wave goodbye to everyone and rush home, hoping I could still remember the song that had been going around my head all night. I would get home with these straight-up jams going on and I would mess around with them for a few more hours.

It was on one of those occasions when I got home and messed around with the tune that had been in my head that I thought I had really hit on something. I was that enthused by it that I called up Curtis McClain, Rudy Forbes and Thomas Carr, who I worked with at the post office. I'm pumped up and say to each of them 'Hey man I've got a cut, you need to hear this'.

I'm getting really excited as I start to lay down the various parts. Studio costs were very expensive so I just did what I usually did and that was record the whole song at home using my own equipment. I recorded all the parts of the song on my Yamaha QX1. I did the piano part and the strings part on a Prophet 2000 and the bass sound was created using my Roland JXP and for the drums I used a Roland 707. Everything was sequenced. I played everything.

I still needed to go into a studio so I took my song to a guy I knew called Lito Manlucu. He had an okay studio. My boys Curtis, Rudy and Thomas came down too. I wanted Curtis to sing the lead vocal and Rudy and Thomas the backing vocals. It only took about fifteen minutes to record the music because it was pretty much all done and then we started to work on recording the vocals.

The guys got into the vocals recording booth and I joined them, so I'm singing on the song too. Rudy did the deep bass lines and me, Tom and Curtis did the higher parts.

Rudy had some musical experience. He also wrote songs and he played keyboards but he wasn't into House music at this time. In fact I don't think he knew anything about House music at all. He looked like a black version of Groucho Marx with his big nose, his glasses and his moustache and he was going bald. Rudy was a good guy and he just wanted to make music and he knew that I was making music and had my Virgo stuff out and, when I told him that we were going to make a record and get us out of the post office, he'd jumped at the opportunity. Rudy had some good songs too and we messed around with songs called *Got To Go* and *Show Me The Way To Your Heart*.

Thomas filled in the gaps we needed with his vocals. Now Tom was a big man. He must have been about six foot five and twenty stone. A big dude! Tom liked to talk to women but when he did he would rhyme the words. He didn't call it rapping. Instead he liked to call it roping because he said he would reel the women with his rhymes. He'd say stuff like 'Baby, I'll invite you over for breakfast brunch, lunch and dinner and anyone you choose will come out a winner' or 'I'm the ace of spades and the king of hearts and in the deck you'll find no joker. I'll wreck your mind, rub on your behind and thrill you with the ropa dopa'. The thing was that even with all of those rhymes, none of us can actually recall Thomas getting any girlfriends. He could make the women laugh but I don't think he closed many deals. He was fun to listen to, a really colourful character, and at the post office everybody loved him.

The thing was that even with all of those rhymes none of us can actually recall Thomas getting any girlfriends. He could make the women laugh but I don't think he closed many deals. He was fun to listen to and a really colourful character and at the post office everybody loved him and many of us learnt his rhymes too.

In the studio Tom would always have to do something to make himself stand out. Just blending in wasn't good enough for him. What Tom needed to be able to do was point out his part to people. On *Move Your Body* while everyone is on the level when they sing their part 'move your body, move your body' what Tom does is to add more emphasis on the 'move' part. But to be fair we all tried to break off at some points to do our own thing. Really we were just a bunch of fools doing background vocals in some studio on some song. But it all worked to make the song what it was.

> *Gotta have house music, all night long*
> *With that house music, you can't go wrong*
> *Give me that house music, set me free*
> *Lost in house music, is where I wanna be*

And then it went on 'It's gonna set you free, rock your body' which goes around a few times before heading into 'move your body' and 'shake your body' and 'move your sexy body'.

I wrote the lyrics to *Move Your Body* on that day in the studio. At the time the other guys weren't really that familiar with House music and what was needed. They certainly got it after *Move Your Body* came out and got real popular.

Alongside me, Curtis, Rudy and Tom there was the guy who owned the studio and his name was Lito. Lito was also the engineer in the studio. He charged me thirty-five dollars an hour for the use of the studio. We recorded two mixes of the song, one with the kick drum boosted and another with the piano more upfront and I think we left the studio after about three hours.

Right away The Dude told me not to let anyone hear it. I thought we'd recorded the jam of all times and I planned on letting everyone hear it. I was really excited about what we'd done and felt like we'd made the greatest song ever and that there was going to be a House Music Hall of Fame and I was going to be the first inductee.

That Prophet 200 keyboard played an essential part in the making of *Move Your Body*. That piano sounded real. At the time nobody had put piano on a House track. Nobody! The idea for using a piano stemmed from the love I had for Elton John's early songs. When I was a kid I wanted to be able to play the piano just like Elton. Back in the 70s Elton John was the coolest man on the planet; he played like a southern-black-just-finished-eating-grits-church-piano-playing FOOL. Yes, Elton John was a black man in the 70s and he even played on Soul Train. The stuff that Elton John and Bernie Taupin did together was the most awesome deep shit ever.

Before *Move Your Body* I had messed around with that piano sound on the Prophet 2000 but I would play it at a much slower speed and then I would speed it up in the mix. I would play at forty beats per minute and then speed it up to one twenty beats but, on *Move Your Body,* I played it at sixty beats and then sped it up to one twenty.

The Yamaha QX1 that I had had a function where you could lengthen all the notes in your song at the same time. This was vital because when you speed something up it sounds very choppy and robotic. The note-lengthening function made everything sound natural. A lot of my friends saw what I was doing and figured they were smarter than me and started doing the same and what do you know? They *did* do it and they started doing records too.

The Yamaha QX1 that I had had a function where you could lengthen all the notes in your song at the same time. This was vital because when you speed something up it sounds very choppy and robotic. The note-lengthening function made everything sound natural. A lot of my friends saw what I was doing and figured they were smarter than me and do the same and what do you know? They *did* do it and they started doing records too.

About a decade after the song came out, I was in Germany and a famous classical pianist wanted to meet me and talk about playing. I was scared to death because I couldn't really play. When we finally hooked up, I immediately told him that I couldn't really play like that and it was all technology. He was very surprised and told me that normally keyboard players wouldn't play like that because it wasn't safe. Normally a pianist would keep his hands in one place and move a few fingers. This meant he could chill and take his eyes off the keyboard, wink at the women and whatever. My parts had the whole hand flying all over the keyboard and were pretty reckless.

When *Move Your Body* was finished I took it to a club called Sheba Baby. There were three DJs that played there: Mike Dunn, Tyree Cooper and Hugo Hutchinson. Those guys went on to become famous producers but back then they were just starting out. At that time I was into my nickname Virgo and everyone called me that. Ron Hardy was playing at least ten of my songs, a lot of them still unreleased so I was an underground star in the Chicago House scene. I let them hear a recording of *Move Your Body*. They all said it was 'jamming' and 'happening' but they didn't seem that excited about it and they certainly didn't give me the response that I thought I'd get. But I left them with the cassette anyway and went on my way.

I next went down to the Music Box to play the song to Ron Hardy. I sat in my car outside the club with K'Alexi who is now a DJ in his own right and a couple of other guys and I played them *Move Your Body*. They said they thought it was nice but again they didn't seem that excited about it. It got me thinking and I couldn't understand why all those guys were not jumping up and down about the song. I still felt it was the jam of all time.

But I took the cassette into the Music Box and I gave the song to Ron. At the time the club was open and the party is going on. Ron takes the cassette from me and puts it straight into the cassette player and presses the on button. He's listening to *Move Your Body* through his headphones and I watch him as his head starts to bob. I start to grin because I can see that he is really getting into the song. The record he had been playing starts to end so what Ron does is he puts *Move Your Body* on as the next record. At first people didn't know what to make of it but as I watch on I can see them starting to get into it and get dancing.

The next thing Ron tosses on a sound effects record which allows him time to rewind the cassette with *Move Your Body* and then he plays the song again. This time people went crazy. I sat back thinking: yeah, that was the response that I was expecting.

After *Move Your Body* had finished a second time Ron throws on yet another sound effects records so that he can rewind the cassette again and then he plays *Move Your Body* again. Ron repeated this four more times and the people in the Music Box that night heard *Move Your Body* become the hottest song in the city.

In no time at all *Move Your Body* blew up and at that time the Music Box was only place where people could hear the song. I next took the song down to Trax Records and I handed Larry Sherman fifteen hundred dollars telling him that I wanted to press some copies of the song. I played Larry the song and his response was 'That's not House music'. By then he figured that he was some kind of authority on House music because he'd put out records by Farley and Adonis and DJ International had also used him to press up some copies of their stuff too – so he really did consider himself to be an expert on the subject of House music and House music didn't have piano in it and it just didn't sound like any other House records. This was also despite the fact that I had Curtis

McClain singing 'gotta have house music all night long'. What Larry couldn't understand was that I had wanted to make a record that didn't sound like anything made by Jesse Saunders or Chip E or Farley. I wanted hot, underground and me, with a focus on being different from everyone else. They had their thing and it was great, but I wanted my own vibe. I was so arrogant back then that I thought I would change everything, that I could expand the genre with every song. Of course I actually wound up almost doing exactly that, isn't that wild? Larry did agree to press up *Move Your Body*. I mean I had handed him the dollars anyway. But he sat on the tape for about nine months. I was forever going down to Precision trying to motivate him to press the record up. During that time the song blew up. Today you would call it going viral. It blew up in Ron Hardy's Music Box first. Ron asked me for an exclusive and not to give it to anyone else, and I agreed because by then he was playing a ton of my stuff. Sleezy had other ideas though and he wanted to get in Frankie Knuckles Power Plant free, so he gave Frankie a copy.

Back then Frankie Knuckles and Ron Hardy tapes would circulate around the city and kids would make copies of copies of copies and when the smoke cleared hundreds of thousands of kids would hear Ronny and Frankie tapes. So now I had Ron Hardy and Frankie Knuckles playing *Move Your Body* in their clubs. Next Frankie passed on a cassette with *Move Your Body* onto his best friend back in New York, Larry Levan. So now you had Ron Hardy, Frankie Knuckles and Larry Levan playing *Move Your Body*. Larry's Paradise Garage nights back then had record distributers and DJs actually flying to New

York from all over the world to hear his playlist. Today the internet solves that problem but then we were prehistoric.

Somehow DJ Jazzy M back in the UK heard *Move Your Body* too and he started playing it on LWR, which was a pirate radio station in London first called London Weekend Radio and then London Wide Radio. Other DJs like Pete Tong, Danny Rampling, Mike Pickering and even Alfredo in Ibiza then got hold of copies too and they all played it and people in the UK started to really ask what the fuck is this House music? I mean *Move Your Body* had the words 'got to have house music all night long' repeated throughout it and the word House was really catching people's attention.

Jazzy M, real name Michael Schiniou would call me up from London and we would talk for hours at a time. Some of our conversations would last three or more hours, on his dime. His phone bill must have solved the national debt. We'd talk all things House music and about guys like Jamie Principle, Farley, Chip, Larry heard, Adonis and Steve Hurley. I would send him tapes of all the stuff and by the time I got out there in 1987, everyone was already familiar with all the songs, so thanks Jazzy.

So the song was blowing up in Chicago, New York and all over the UK and I also had a woman named Abigail Adams from Moving Records in New Jersey calling me up every day; she was also big into House music. How she found out about me and got my number I have no idea, but she was on it. Abby would also talk for hours on the phone and I wondered how the hell she was running her business.

Somehow, Frankie Knuckles found out about the scene exploding and went to the UK to represent House music. He quickly got the Godfather of House Music title even though he didn't have any records out yet. This was quickly solved by Trax records, who slapped his name on Jamie Principal's *Your Love*. Benji Espinoza from DJ International had contacted a bunch of music journalists from the UK and he'd arranged for them to come out to Chicago to meet some of us House people and investigate House music. At the time there were only two records, *Jack Trax* by Chip E and *Move Your Body* by me, that actually mentioned House music.

Benji handled the marketing and promotional side of DJ International and Rocky Jones was the head of it. Lauren Alcarez, who was Rocky's sister also worked at DJ International and she handled the clerical work.

Benji arranged a bunch of meetings in various places all over Chicago and I would go and meet with them. I would usually see one at a time but Benji then organised for them all to come and see me in the Paradigm Recording studios where I was doing a remix of *Move Your Body*.

I had wanted to do a different mix of *Move Your Body* because I thought I could do better. Wrong. First of all, my boys from the post office saw all the British reporters and that immediately changed their perspectives. Nobody could sing background vocals. If you listen to that DJ International version today you'll hear a mess of soloing by everyone instead of the background vocals.

There was also a pretty fucked version of *Move Your Body* going around too that had been done by Rocky Jones.

Somehow he'd got his hands on a copy of the original multi-track recording that I had. In fact Rocky still has that tape to this day.

Back in 1986 Rocky said he'd give me a contract offering to pay me three thousand dollars a month but that never happened. I was in the studio doing a mix of *Move Your Body* and all these UK reporters were watching and talking to me. Rocky was also still on my case asking me when I was going to sign the contract, to which I would reply as soon as you give me my first three thousand dollars.

Rocky never gave me the money but kept the tape and put it out on DJ International.

Larry Sherman got wind of all the reporters in town and quickly injected himself into Chicago House lore, which he deserved. He arranged to take the reporters to the top House clubs in the city and show them the House scene. He was still at that time ignoring my pleas to press up *Move Your Body* on my label and had no idea of its popularity until he took the press around to the clubs and heard all the DJ's playing *Move Your Body* on cassette and seeing the crowds go wild.

That DJ International version of *Move Your Body* was pretty much like a live performance where the guys and me were just showing off. We were all there: Curtis, Rudy and Tom and we're all trying to grab the attention of the journalists. So we're playing the song and man, we really fucked it up. There were no background vocals because everyone was competing to be up front. Everybody just sang their own shit and it was shit. But DJ International pressed up copies anyway.

When the record came out, first on Trax, the label read *The House Music Anthem*. It was my suggestion to call the song that because I was pissed off that so many people still didn't consider it to be a House music record. I thought I'll call it *The House Music Anthem* and fuck all of you.

The song does well in Chicago, New York and all over the UK and I also have a woman called Abigail Adams from Moving Record Store in New Jersey is calling me up every day too; she was also big into House music. With all this positive feedback about the song I had to put pressure on Larry to get the song pressed up and, like I say, he did in the end and what helped was when those UK journalists went to see Larry down at Trax Records. Of course he loved all the attention and told those guys about he knows everything about House music and that it's him who presses up and puts out all the House music in Chicago.

What he next does is to take these journalists to some of the main House clubs in Chicago. Larry gets the VIP treatment at these places because he's the white guy with the record company. During those visits to the clubs what Larry discovers is that the whole of Chicago is playing *Move Your Body* on cassette.

The journalists heard *Move Your Body* getting played and told Larry that it was also being played back in London. That's when Larry starts to see dollar signs. That night that motherfucker pressed up my song.

Now, the other thing was when I had first taken *Move Your Body* to Larry I wanted it pressed up on my record label which was Other Side Records – the label that *Virgo Go Wild* had been issued on. But Larry pressed it up as a Trax Records product without my agreeing to it.

The record was also supposed to be released by the artist On The House – which was Rudy, Curtis, Tom and myself and the production credit was going to go to Virgo. But it came out as a *The House Music Anthem* by Marshall Jefferson and produced by Virgo. What this mistake also did was ruin my name Virgo. After that record came out I couldn't be Virgo anymore, I had to be Marshall Jefferson. So Larry fucked that up for me too. I loved that name Virgo and everybody was calling me it – Frankie, Ron, Lil Louis everybody. I was really pissed off. My whole life I wanted to be known by a nickname and I found one that I loved but then I had to go back to being called Marshall Jefferson again. Man, I was pissed!

The next problem I had to deal with once the record came out was with Curtis, Rudy and Tom because their names weren't on the record. All they saw was my name on the label. They were pissed and very angry and they called me up. I tried to tell them what had happened and that it was not my fault or my intention to cut them out. But at first they didn't believe me and all their thinking is that I'm just some sort of egomaniac.

When they came over to my place I could see that they were really pissed off with me so I produced a copy of the label that I had written out and given to Larry. This label included all the information about On The House and their names. But even by producing that label they still didn't believe me so I told them to go and see Larry and see for themselves.

Curtis, Tom and Rudy then went to see Larry but he basically tells them that all he sees is Marshall Jefferson's name on the record and they can kiss his ass and get out or he'll call the cops. They then come back to see me and tell me what had happened.

Now Curtis knew a guy called Norman Davis and he came up with the idea for me to sign an affidavit saying that Curtis, Rudy and Tom sang on the record. Of course I agreed to that and I signed it and they took it with them to show Larry. Larry's response to them was that he only put my name on the record because I had signed a contract with him and Trax Records for the song and he added that he also gave me one hundred and fifty thousand dollars.

Now Curtis, Rudy and Tom know I'm living in some crappy apartment on the West Side, two doors down from Fast Eddie and a block from Lil Louis, but they come back to me yelling about some contract and that I'd gotten $150,000 but I ask them to look around and say, 'Do you really think that if Larry Sherman gave me one hundred and fifty thousand dollars I would be living in this lap of luxury?' For a long time after that they were pretty hostile towards me and I guess I understand, but damn, it hurt.

This was made a lot easier by all the attention I got from *Move Your Body* blowing up. I was famous man! I heard my song on the radio a LOT! I had the hottest dance song in the world and I knew it. I got freebies or discounts everywhere I went. Women were throwing themselves at me and I kept repeating; I love Esther I love Esther I love Esther I love Esther.

Anyway, *Move Your Body* blew up the underground and was *the* hottest song in the clubs. Everyone contacted me for deals but I got one call in particular that was very impressive to me. It was from Jamie Principal, who did *Your Love, Waiting on My Angel, Bad Boys, Baby wants To Ride*, and many other unreleased club hits. Jamie told me that his and Steve's managers were two Italian guys, Phil and Frank, and that I should also hook up with them. Jamie also said that he'd like to work with me but I told him that I loved his stuff but we were two very different producers. I told him that I thought songs like *Your Love* and *Waiting on My Angel* were brilliant but that *Jack Your Body* was just an okay song. I just didn't like the rapid-fire sampled vocal thing man, same with Chip E's stuff. The next thing I know Steve Hurley picks up the phone and starts insulting me and calling my stuff beat tracks. It turned out that when I was talking to Jamie, Frank, the manager, had me on speaker phone and Steve and a few others were listening in. That was some low shit. Sucker put me on speaker. That should have scared me off the situation right there but Frank started talking about major labels and said he was also managing Frankie Knuckles so I decided to bite the bullet and try them out.

This was when *Move Your Body* was out and doing really well. Because the song was doing well we had loads of people wanting to book us to perform the song in the clubs. Larry had also booked us a bunch of shows in New York and on the East Coast, including the Paradise Garage. The problem was we didn't have anything even resembling a show. But Steve 'Silk' Hurley, Butch Moore and Keith Nunnally took our On The

House crew under their wing and showed us how to do a live show. Keith Nunally taught us stage presence, which was the most important thing, because if you forgot your dance steps and everything else, stage presence would carry you. Butch Moore taught us the dance steps. Steve edited a show mix in under an hour, physically cutting the tape himself. We later left Phil and Frank and when they kept our show tapes it took me and two pro engineers over eleven hours to try to duplicate the razor-sharp editing job Steve did.

Me and Curtis for some reason decided to hide the fact that we were DJs and wanted to be known as proper artists, because there was a lack of respect at that time for DJs' musical abilities.

Back to Phil and Frank. They took over all the shows. Larry booked and told everyone the money was going through them. There was a problem, I believe, with people already sending deposits to Larry. The very first show was supposed to be at the Paradise Garage, and it was a big one. At least three of the biggest record pools in the world were sponsoring the party. Ricket's Records, The V.I.P. Record Pool, and For the Record, which was Judy Weinstein's pool. At that time major labels would send free records to record pools to get them to all the major DJs. Well, Larry had met with all the record pool people and gotten them to support everything on Trax records, in exchange for the Paradise Garage party performances. I personally met Bill Ricket, Eddie Rivera and Judy Weinstein at her record pool headquarters, where I also met David Morales.

Of course we agree and we were all set to fly to New York. But on the day Phil and Frank told us to not go. We ended up staying in Chicago. I had a bunch of angry record pool guys calling me up at my house. I couldn't deal with them so I thought, 'Fuck it, I'll go over to Curtis's crib'. But they tracked me down there and kept saying, 'You've got to do the show' and they told me that if I didn't do the show my career would be over because none of the guys in the record pools would play *Move Your Body*.

Those guys really wanted us there. They offered us everything – drugs, drink, women – but we still didn't go. We missed the Paradise Garage show and I thought my music career was over because one of the record pool leaders told me so. He said he would tell DJs not to play anything I did ever again, and that the record pools were united on that.

But *Move Your Body* was so hot that nobody could stop playing it. People started calling and booking us and we finally hit the East Coast.

One of our first live performances was at the Paradise Garage, and it was pretty spectacular. The show itself was pretty good, but backstage we saw Eddie Murphy, Taimak, who starred in the movie *The Last Dragon*, Melissa Morgan, Robert De Niro, and Mike Tyson, among other celebrities. I actually had a long conversation with Mike Tyson and Curtis had a long talk with Taimak. Although Eddie Murphy and Robert De Niro just politely said "wassup" and shook my hand, I was still pretty thrilled. I also saw my future girlfriend Tina Graham in the front row. So that worked out well down the line.

Our next shows were in New Jersey, but let me explain something about the New York/New Jersey club scene back then. It was all Mafia controlled and financed. Money was laundered through the clubs but no expense was spared with club quality. There were separate sound systems for the live acts and the DJs, all by Richard Long. Spectacular professional lighting for live acts. Mandatory limousines. DJ's had to spin the whole night, but it was *their* club, and they would get at least $1000 a night but most would get $3000 or even higher. It really was a magical time for smaller acts like mine and there was nothing like it in the world before or since.

Then in 1987, the IRS cracked down on the Mafia and all the money laundering. I estimate at least 300 clubs bit the dust. Since then, I can count on one hand how many sound systems are separated for DJs and live acts; a lot of times they just plug the singer into the DJ mixer with no effects and tell them to go for it. No more limos either, they either tell us to catch a cab or get one of their boys to pick us up. And now the resident DJ is getting maybe $50 a night, and this is at big clubs.

Anyway, we played at a club called Sensations, in Newark. The club was packed, but as we walked to the stage, we heard people telling us "Y'all *BETTER* be good". To say the crowd seemed hostile is an understatement. We didn't have iPhones back then, I wanted to call my mother and tell her I loved her and goodbye.

When *Move Your Body* came on and Curtis sang that first line, it was all over. There was screaming and cheering and hands-in-the-air. When we finished there was woofing; which at that time was the ghetto standing ovation.

We next played at Club 88, in East Orange, which was run by Billie Prest. Much more civilized crowd and we tore the roof off that place too. Billie gave us first class treatment and gave us a private limo to go around town in to wherever we wanted. We went everywhere too. I also met Bridget, the Hostess With The Mostest. Yes, Grammarly, that's how you spell it. Bridget had a prodigious cleavage and later became my girlfriend.

We also played at The Red Parrot in New York, a huge club with Gayle "Sky" King DJ'ing. She had the crowd singing along with almost every song. Eric B and Rakim opened for us; it was just before they got famous so they had a mediocre crowd response. Everyone wanted to hear *Move Your Body* and we blew the roof off. Later Eric B had beat up a bouncer. You know Eric B was a big motherfucker if he was beating up bouncers man. He could've whooped any ass in that club including mine, but he took on a bouncer. Don't mess with Eric B. The club brought the bouncer backstage and made him apologize to Eric. I was expecting Eric to say "It's all good" or something but he stuck his finger in the bouncer's face and said "don't you EVER say some shit like that to me again!"

I also made it to a club called Hearthrob, with DJ Little Louie Vega spinning. It was predominantly Latino and we tore the roof off. Louie was awesome but at that time he was playing mostly freestyle music, much different from the House that he played later on.

New York was conquered, and we headed back to Chicago. We had a road manager with us named Evans

Hightower. Evans had collected all the money from all the shows. When we got back to Chicago, he handed all the money to Phil and Frank. We never saw it.

Frank showed us two checkbooks. One said "Marshall Jefferson" and the other said "On The House" which I assumed was for Curt and Rudy. Thomas decided not to tour with us. Well, I didn't open the account and I had no access to it. And why did Frank have the checkbooks? I asked Frank about all this and he exploded, saying that if we didn't act more professional we'd never get a major label deal. I noticed Frank had by far the highest seat in the room and deduced that he'd obviously read some books on power perception in business. What Frank didn't know was I'd read the same books, so I got out of my seat, walked up to his desk and stood over him. I saw him visibly shrink once I did this; he was so into power that when I flipped the script on him he was out of his comfort zone.

A few days later Frank called me and Curtis into his office and told us Rudy wasn't professional; he kept asking for money. Rudy was married with a kid, so I told Frank to give him whatever he asked for and I wanted my money too. ALL of it. Frank lost it again and came up with a bunch of reasons why getting taking our money was a bad idea, but I'd had enough. I said "Give us our money right now. All 35,000 of it, or we're walking." Frank didn't give us our money, and we walked. Keith Nunally found out and I told him Frank had kept $35,000 of our money. Keith, Steve, and JM Silk and been touring more than a year before us; if we got $35,000 in one weekend, imagine how much of Keith and Steve's money they were holding. The next thing I hear, Keith has left too. Steve stayed. I know Keith told him why he left so I was puzzled. Anyway, ten years later I had a conversation with Steve and he told me Frank had gotten him for millions before he left.

We were free from Phil and Frank, so DeWayne Powell took over. We had months of gigs and DeWayne took over coordinating our bookings. Norman Davis became our new road manager and we set off for the East Coast again. On our last trip we met a guy named Kaif. Kaif asked us if he could help carry our equipment around to all the gigs for free, and of course we said ok. Kaif would always bring beautiful girls backstage and introduce them to us. This went on for a few weeks before we realized Kaif would quickly take the women out of the dressing room after introducing them to us and fuck them himself. Kaif even got a friend to help him carry our stuff and the friend did the same thing, so we cut them loose before Kaif brought even more guys.

We played a gigantic club called 1018, with Roman Ricardo spinning. It was another Latino/Freestyle club and of course we ripped that club up too. Backstage was Brenda K Starr, a stunning singer that was just hanging out with her girlfriend, Mariah Carey. They were very beautiful girls and Brenda was doing all the talking because she was already a star, we never got a chance to talk to Mariah because she was unknown at the time and we were whisked off to another gig we had the same night.

We also played at the Cheetah Club, with Tee Scott spinning. Tee was so great that I stayed after the gig to listen to his set. At the bar I met a beautiful girl named Dana who later became Queen Latifah. She was very friendly, told me she loved my stuff and a lot of other House Music, and that she'd just signed a record deal. I couldn't get out of the friend zone though, I guess she had me pegged as a player and kept me at a distance. She was fine at that time though. Woo, not too skinny but not big either-just right. A lot of famous people look really skinny when you see them in person, almost like skeletons. Cameras put a lot of weight on you, so they have to stay at that weight. It's a real shame.

We played at The Latin Quarter in Manhattan, which was a Hip Hop club. The crowd was pretty hostile at first, when we walked towards the stage, we heard people shouting "Get That House Music shit out of here!" Of course when *Move Your Body* came on, all the hostility flew out the window.

So we'd conquered Hip Hop and Freestyle clubs with impunity and thought we were invincible. Armed with *Move Your Body* we felt we could blow away any crowd on the planet. We seriously believed that if Michael Jackson performed at the same club as us, we'd blow him off the stage. That's how confident we were.

Finally, we played at Zanzibar, where Tony Humphries was the DJ. Billie Prest ran Zanzibar also, so we knew were going to get first class treatment. Joe Smooth was there that night performing *Going Down* with Anthony Thomas. Anthony did sensational vocals but the crowd wasn't into it, they were there to hear Move Your Body. Likewise for Wally

Jump jr. who got booed. Will Downing was the vocalist. I also met my good friend Carolyn Byrd, an unforgettable character.

Billie gave us a limo again to do with as we saw fit, and we hit some clubs cruising for women. At one of the clubs that Billie managed called America I met Miss Happy, who I'll get to later.

Anyway, a great time was had by me and the boys, and just before we left Billie gave a me a cassette of a singer he was managing named Ce Ce Rogers. I listened to it when I got to Chicago and told Billie I had a song called *Someday* for Ce Ce to sing. I sent him a demo with my vocals on it in the mail- it took a few days, and Billie said he was flying Ce Ce to Chicago within the next few days. I booked a session at Streeterville in Chicago; Steve Frisk was the engineer, who I'd worked with before, and Billie paid for the flights and the studio time. Now Ce Ce Rogers was a graduate from Berkely College Of Music and a virtuoso level keyboard player, and I later learned that Billie specifically told him not to play keyboards in front of me because he didn't want to destroy my confidence. Not a chance. My ego is unbreakable.

I guess Ce Ce was initially willing to stick to the plan, but I had women in the studio-Angie and her sister Niecy, and both had big boobs of course. Turns out Ce Ce was a boob man too and within seconds after entering the studio that fat sucker pounced on the first grand piano he saw and started playing like his life depended on it. The girls were swooning of course but the show wasn't over-he still hadn't sang yet.

I told Ce Ce to warm up and sing the song all the way through to practice, telling Steve on the sly to record everything. Ce Ce was practicing, but like I said there were women in the studio-big boobed women at that.

That "practice run" was the greatest vocal performance I've ever heard on a record. One take. Boom. I knew it would bring tears to the eyes of many people. Angie and Niecy were already crying. I couldn't believe how great a singer and performer this dude was.

"Okay, I'm ready to start". Me and Steve are laughing because we know we recorded it, then I turn around to tell the girls and they start laughing too. I told Ce Ce we recorded it and it was a wrap, he could go back home.

Then I heard the most ridiculous thing ever in my music career; "Let me sing it again" Me and Steve look at each other, puzzled. "I can do it better, let me fix it"

I spend a few minutes trying to talk him out of it but no use-he's set on doing it. So I told Steve to guard the first take with his life, and I went to McDonalds. When I came back Ce Ce had done three more takes, but none as good as the first and I felt his voice was getting progressively weaker with each take, so I shut down the session.

Ce Ce even flew out a second time to do the vocals after he'd signed with Atlantic Records, but we all agreed the first take was still the magical one and that's what came out on record.

CHAPTER SIX

Marshall Jefferson has been one of the most consistent and prolific creators of music of our time and he is a genuinely a super nice person. He has helped me to see the way music should be done. Love and respect for my big brother – always!
K Alexi Shelby

Frankie Knuckles had started deejaying at the new club, Powerhouse, which Phil and Frank owned. They also told Frankie that they wanted him to be the club's main DJ. Frankie agreed and the club opened and Frankie's crowd followed him there, because everyone thought it was Frankie's club. Frankie took his own equipment to the club: decks, mixers, his reel to reel machine and so on. Of course whatever Frankie did was going to work and the club was a huge success.

The thing was Phil and Frank made the mistake of thinking that the people were going to the club because they liked the club and it had nothing to do with Frankie. So they fired Frankie, which must have been particularly humiliating to Frankie because everyone thought it was his club. The Powerhouse had only been open a few months max by this point. Within two weeks, when everyone found out Frankie was no longer spinning there, the club was completely empty.

The first night when Frankie wasn't going to DJ he'd gone back to the club to retrieve his equipment. But Phil and Frank wouldn't let Frankie back into the club and basically told him to fuck off. Frankie didn't take too kindly to this and went and got the cops. They all went into the club and started to argue over the equipment. Frankie was telling the cops that the decks and everything were his and Phil and Frank were telling the cops that the equipment was theirs. But what Phil and Frank didn't expect was for Frankie to produce all the receipts and serial numbers for every single piece of equipment that he'd taken into the Power House. Frankie walked away from that club with all of his equipment.

The Power House only lasted for a couple more months after Frankie was gone. That club plays its part in the history of Chicago House music, but there are not many people that have even heard of it or know its story.

1987 was a year where some great House records got released. Take a track like *Your Love*. Frankie had been playing that song at the Power Plant since around 1983/84. *Your Love* had been written by a Chicago guy called Jamie Principle; he'd also written *Bad Boy* and *Waiting on my Angel*, which were also huge House hits.

Jamie was a singer and a musician. He sang and played all the instruments on those tracks that people know him for. He wasn't really into going to the various House clubs in Chicago and I remember that he was a big fan of Prince. He just loved to make songs from his bedroom. His music was put onto cassette and somehow Frankie got hold of one and he started to play *Your Love* in the Power Plant. Frankie would also play Jamie's other songs and the crowds were going wild for them. By contrast Ron Hardy was playing my songs in his club and people were going wild for them too and Ron played my stuff alongside Jamie's, and people went really wild.

Jamie and I became friends and today we remain very good friends. I remember that when I first heard his music I thought he was European. Jamie was a quiet guy, he certainly wasn't an overwhelming character like say Farley or to some extent me. Jamie is the kind of guy who enters a room and just blends in.

Now Phil and Frank enter the story again at this point because right after Frankie Knuckles got all of his shit back from the Power House I heard that they threatened to fuck Frankie up and made claims again that they were connected to the Mafia.

What Frankie did was to take Jamie's songs to Larry Sherman and he sold them for an undisclosed amount of money. Frankie needed the money because he wanted to get out of Chicago and go to New York and then there'd be some distance between him and the two Italian managers, Phil and Frank, because they frequently hinted that they were connected to the Mafia. Those guys must have said something to Frankie that really spooked him because he packed up and left pretty quickly.

So Frankie sold Jamie's songs to Larry Sherman and this meant that he could release them at his discretion on Trax Records, but Jamie didn't know anything about the deal. Trax went onto release tracks like *Your Love* and Frankie got the credit for those songs and not Jamie.

I love Jamie's songs. It was some of Jamie's songs that I sent to Jazzy M back in the day and he just flipped over them. He helped to break those songs because he played them on LWR.

Once Frankie had safely gotten to New York he hooked up with Judy Weinstein and another guy, whose name I now forget and they were opening up a new club in Manhattan's East Village called the World. That club became very popular and a bit of a celebrity hang-out place. People like Prince and Madonna would often frequent the place and during the club's life there were live performances too from David Bowie and The Beastie Boys.

This guy who was involved with the World was also Italian and it was rumoured that he was also connected to the Mafia so it was assumed the he could offer Frankie protection from the guys back in Chicago. As time passed Frankie was okay and it was also revealed that Phil and Frank really weren't that connected to the Mafia at all or, if they were, it was only minimal and they really didn't have much power at all. The World closed in 1991 after the owner was found dead on the floor of the club.

I remember playing at The World one night with Ce Ce Rogers and Screamin Rachael. We met Prince backstage; I shook his hand and he said one word to me; "Purple". We're about to go on stage and I'm wondering "wtf is purple?" Can this motherfucker speak in sentences like normal people? But I was told about a year later by a limo driver that Prince could see auras on people, and purple was the aura of greatness. The limo driver said he could see auras too, and sure enough I was a purple. He also said the only other purples he'd met in his life were James Brown and George Clinton. Yeah, right. I think he may have drunk too much purple rain.

Jungle Wonz came after meeting Harry Dennis. The first song that we did together was *The Jungle*, which came out in 1986. Harry recited the worlds to me and I thought it was deep as hell, so I did some music to it. It worked great for me because I really didn't like working on music with people, because I pretty much saw the song finish before I even sat down at a keyboard, and somebody else pecking away at the keyboard and adding their vision would screw everything up.

With Harry it was him: words, me: music and that suited me just fine.

Harry next brought me the words to *Time Marches On* and I thought it was even better than *The Jungle*, so I had to come up with san even deeper.

We recorded *The Jungle* and *Time Marches On* at the Italian managers', Phil and Frank's studio. A few House people used their studio including some of the DJ International guys. We went into that studio around February March time 1986 and it was after that when Phil and Frank contacted me through Jamie saying they wanted to manage me.

We recorded and mixed *Time Marches On* in four hours.

Time Marches On was issued on Trax TX135 in 1987 and their very next release was *Give Me Back The Love* which I did under On The House and that was TX136. On The House actually recorded an entire album in 1986. That album has never been released. In fact, during that period a lot of songs that I was involved in just got lost.

On The House was me, Curtis McClain, Rudy Forbes and Thomas Carr. his was the group that did *Move Your Body, Pleasure Control, Ride The Rhythm, Give Me Back The Love, and Let's Get Busy.*

The same year that I was doing Jungle Wonz and On The House I also did the Marshall Jefferson Presents Hercules stuff. *Lost in the Groove* was the first release and I did that song with a guy I had got to know called Michael Smith. Now Michael was a big motherfucker and a big dude and that's how he got the nickname Hercules, which we'd shorten to Herc.

Herc and me would hang out and I just got the idea in my head that he should also be famous on the House scene, so I took him into the studio. The first song we actually did was *Seven Ways to Jack.* That track was issued on Dance Mania Records, which was another of Jesse Saunders' record labels. But there was a problem encountered during the making of *Seven Ways to Jack.* Once in the studio and once the mic was put in front of Herc, he froze up. His nerves got the better of him and he just couldn't get the words out. The way we got around this meant that I ended up saying all the words which I had written.

Seven ways I'm going to move your soul
Seven ways we're going to lose control
Seven ways we'll give no slack
Seven ways to make you jack

When *Seven Ways to Jack* was released we still did it as a Hercules song, even though he didn't sing on it. I did take Herc back into the studio for *Lost in the Groove* and he did sing on that record. We used a harmonizer on his vocals which made him sound a lot lower and that suited the song. By that time he also had a lot more confidence because *Seven Ways to Jack* was getting played in the clubs and Herc was getting a lot of attention from the girls. *Lost in the Groove* was released on Trax with the B-side being *Lost in House Mix* and *Groove Appella*.

1987 was also the year that I worked with Phuture on their *Acid Tracks* record. When Trax released the record it was credited as produced and mixed by Marshall Jefferson.

Before I met the Phuture guys Ron Hardy had given me a cassette with *Acid Tracks* on it. I thought it was an awesome track. In fact so impressed was I by it I took it to Larry Sherman and told him that he needed to put it on Trax. I took it to Larry because around that time I was really trying to push Trax as being the underground House music record label.

Three years before I had done a song with Sleezy called *I've Lost Control*. It had a Roland TB303 on it and a weird bassline, because I didn't really understand how to program it. So when Ron Hardy gave me a cassette copy of *Acid Tracks*, it was right up my alley. I called up Pierre on the phone and he said he wanted to put it out on Trax. I agreed to talk to Larry for him and I took the Phuture guys into the studio, which was owed by one of my best friends in grammar school, Kevin Clay. Once in the studio they did it all. The thing was they already had the song. They knew every part and they knew exactly what they needed to do and when to do it. I literally just sat back and watched them do their thing.

There was nothing around like *Acid Tracks*. It had that squelchy sound going on and it really sucked you in. Larry listened to it and he agreed to release it on Trax only if I put my name to it as being the producer. I agreed and I took the Phuture guys into the studio. Once in the studio they did it all. The thing was they already had the song. They knew every part and they knew exactly what they needed to do and when to do it. I literally just sat back and watched them do their thing.

Phuture was made up of Nathaniel Pierre Jones, better known simply as DJ Pierre, Herb J and Spanky, real name Earl Smith Jnr. Spanky sadly died after suffering from a stroke in 2016 aged just fifty-one years old. In the studio they worked perfectly together. One turned a knob to make that sound and another turned a knob to create another sound and another worked the drum machine and the result was eleven minutes and seventeen seconds of what many consider to be the first acid house record.

I recall a conversation I had with Herb where he told me that the inspiration for *Acid Tracks* came from listening to *I've Lost Control*. He said that sound made by the TB-303 had just blown him away. We talked about the bassline I had made and how, because I didn't really know how to work the machine, it had come out sounding all wack.

The real credit for the production of *Acid Tracks* should go to Phuture because it really was them and I had very little to do on it. I watched on while they recorded their whole EP which also included the brilliant *Your Only Friend*. Well, actually, I told Spanky to say "This is cocaine speaking".

Once the record hit the UK the press there really jumped on it. Back in Chicago we weren't calling it acid house; that was a name that the press in the UK started to push and they knew they could have a field day with that. I didn't really have much of an opinion about the term. It didn't really matter to me what they called it. As time went on and I worked with more people like Kym Mazelle or Ce Ce Rogers or Ten City they started to call my music all sorts of names like Deep House or New Jersey House. I really didn't think too much on it, though.

Because of *Move Your Body* people in the House world knew who I was. I hooked up with a girl called Cynthia at some party and she said that she wanted to work with me. She told me that she was a very good singer. Kym was also there and she said she could sing a little bit too. I was also at the party with my lawyer DeWayne Powell and, after listening to Cynthia, I told to DeWayne I was going to take Cynthia and Kym into the studio.

The idea was that Cynthia would do the lead vocal and Kym would do some backing vocals on a song I had called *Taste My Love*. At this stage Kym was very shy and didn't say much.

So we recorded Kym's backing vocals first and she did it all the way through with no problems, no mistakes, one take on each part, and they were incredible. I was really impressed and thought I'd keep this girl in mind for the future. Next up was Cynthia. We put her in front of the microphone and she totally fucks up. We discover very quickly that she can't sing for shit. I'm looking at the engineer and he's looking back at me and we're both mouthing, 'What the fuck?'

DeWayne was also listening and he tells me that maybe Cynthia just needs some time to learn the song, but I just told him no thanks, we're getting the girl that sang the backgrounds to do the leads. So DeWayne handles that and I ask Kym to sing the lead vocals on the song instead.

At the time Kym was still using her real name Kimberly Grigsby and she was very nerdy looking with glasses and she was what I would call 'healthy'-looking, which means not too much but a little overweight, and she had gigantic boobs. She was so shy back then but nowadays she can't stop talking. She always has something interesting to say and she's family so it's ok.

At the time Kym was still using her real name Kimberly Grigsby and she was very nerdy looking with glasses and she was what I would call 'healthy'-looking, which means not too much but a little overweight, and she had gigantic boobs. She was so shy back then but nowadays she can't stop talking. She always has something interesting to say and she's family so it's ok.

Kym and I have been dear friends ever since doing *Taste My Love*. After *Taste My Love* we did another song called *I'm a Lover* which we also recorded. The early songs were put out on Police Records, which was DeWayne Powell's record label. After Kym got signed to EMI records in the U.K. she had a young guy look after her by the name of Simon Cowell.

Man I wish I had known then what I know now, I would've been way better than Randy Jackson.

DeWayne Powell was an attorney. He was black and he was gay. I think he came from somewhere in the Caribbean but he didn't sound like he did. Sterling Void used to call him Poindexter from Felix the Cat. I think Sterling must have thought he reminded him of that character with his big round glasses on and his precise way of talking.

It seemed like every other lawyer in Chicago hated DeWayne. The reason for this was because DeWayne had the ability to call up any of the major record labels and they would take his call and this wasn't the case for a lot of the other guys. So when House music first started jumping off all the established music attorneys were trying to get in on it and get inside the majors but they weren't getting anywhere, but DeWayne was. There were a lot of power struggles around that time with the established music attorneys all ganging up on DeWayne.

I heard a lot of derogatory things said about DeWayne and people would tell me that I shouldn't get involved with DeWayne because he was gay and didn't know what he was doing. All I knew was that DeWayne could get the job done. He'd organise and arrange listening parties for the big guys in the music industry and they would show up and he handled stuff properly. He was also the only black attorney around for guys like us from the House scene, which meant he was the only black person talking for us. DeWayne also handled Kym Mazelle and Lil Louis.

I was with DeWayne Powell for about four years. Our relationship worked for me so that's why I stayed with him. I also became good friends with DeWayne's boyfriend who was Andre Walker. Now Andre was Oprah Winfrey's hairdresser. He helped close a few deals for me because this was also the time where I'm flying all around the world promoting my records and I'm getting a lot of attention from the ladies. And when I brought my various girlfriends into Chicago I would take them to see Andre and he'd do their hair for free and they loved this. Getting their hair done by Oprah's hairdresser? Man! You know I was in good after that. Andre also worked with a lot of celebrities. Whitney Houston was one of them. I think he may still be Oprah's hairdresser.

So a lot of things were going on for me and around me by 1987. I had records out, was travelling all over the world and getting a lot of attention.

I also broke up with Esther. I was pretty stupid and a walking hormone; I was planning on jumping on almost any female with two legs and I didn't want to put her through it. My house got robbed and I moved in with Bam Bam, on 63rd and Artesian, on the edge of Englewood, the most dangerous neighbourhood in America. I didn't want to live by myself because I was going out of town every weekend and needed someone to watch my stuff. Now I grew up on the South side in a nice neighbourhood that had Barack Obama in it, and I moved to the west side which was a pretty bad neighbourhood, even though I lived two doors down from Fast Eddie (who also got robbed), Lil Louis, and Byron Stingily, and finally to

Englewood, which is the worst, most violent area in America. Someone was always at Bam Bam's though. Sherman Burks lived there, Mike Dunn lived there, K'Alexi lived there, Gershon Jackson lived there, Chauncey Alexander lived there, Kim English lived there, and just about all of Chicago's house community would make an appearance at some point. Farley would come over a lot, Terry Hunter too, and Terry would play video games with us and always shout his name at the top of his lungs; "TERRY HUNTER" "THAT'S TERRY HUNTER GITTIN IN YO ASS!!" Armando would come over almost every day, along with Maurice Joshua and Hula Mahome. Reggie Hall would come over when he would break up with his wife. It was tons of fun and ridiculously funny every day; it was literally a joke a minute.

It was a huge house and Bam Bam was the ring leader. Huge ego so we talked about his ass because he could take it. He would bring a different girl home every night from the club and at some point he would always come out of his room and say to one of us very seriously; "I think she's in love with me man". Bam Bam would talk the most shit when we played video games and always lose spectacularly. Sometimes we would play some of the Detroit boys or Mike Hitman Wilsons crew and they would all laugh at Bam when he lost. But they all loved Bam. They wouldn't come over unless they knew Bam was there because they knew it would be a lot of fun.

K'Alexi relegated himself to the basement just so he could call it the dungeon. He would called women on the phone and say "you coming into the dungeon today?" they'd say yes and then he'd ask "are you going to kiss the dragon?" Now we all knew what the dungeon was but we didn't know what the dragon was and nobody had the nerve to ask him. But one hot day in the summer K had his shirt off and bang! I saw a big ass dragon tattoo. Strange things would happen in the dungeon too. I remember one time K had a girl named Cat over and before I could ask what her real name was I heard meowing coming from the dungeon.

Kim English was the heart of the house and nobody touched her. She was also an unbelievably talented singer and songwriter. Ridiculously beautiful too, even when she woke up in the morning. Get your mind out of the gutter, she lived with us and we all saw her! If somebody would have messed with Kim, they would have died quickly.

Gershon was the undisputed funniest guy in the house and things he would say we still repeat now, 30 years later. He also kept the fridge clean because that sucker could eat.

Chauncey was the house instigator, he would do what we called "put the jumper cables on". Whatever you did, he would find something you left out. If you made a salad and used regular tomatoes, he would say 'you really would've set it out if you would've put roma tomatoes in". This would be repeated at least twenty times. Same thing if you did a song and you left out an extra hi hat. Even when we played video games and we'd win, he'd say "you still didn't beat Terry Hunter yet". Then when we'd beat Terry Hunter he'd say; "Well the last time we played I smashed yo ass". Thing is, you could beat Chauncey fifty times and if he beat you the fifty first game, he'd never play you again, just so he could have bragging rights.

Sherman was co-owner of the house with Bam and also military. He also saw how easily I was making music and knew he was more talented than the rest of us so he started making it too. Really good music. I remember shortly after Sherman made his first song he so was proud of it that he got one of his girlfriends over and started slapping her ass to the beat while he was having sex with her. LOUDLY. You see? I couldn't put Esther through that shit! We were animals!

We basically had a house driven by hormones with rotating women every day. And guess what? Mike Dunn was the MAN. We called him Goldie, after the pimp in the movie *The Mack.*

I flew women in from out of town and took them straight to Oprah's hairdresser. I had hit records out. I'm busting out my boys so I may as well include myself. I was a bad man. A whore. I capitalized on my situation. Now that I've gotten the politically correct thing out of the way I must add that I had an absolute ball.

Shortly after moving in with Bam and the crew I went back to New York for a long weekend with Curt and Rudy. We had nine gigs in one weekend so I decided to bring Byron Stingily and Byron Burke with us. I first met Byron down at Trax Records. He was with another guy called Dez and they had a group together called Dez 7. They dressed like Prince and looked like they came straight out of Minneapolis. Byron and Dez actually came from the West Side of Chicago, which was the rough part of town.

I remember listening to a record by Dez 7 called *Funny Love*, the lyrics were awesome. Byron really caught my vibe. When he listened to my music he really understood it. Curt and Rudy didn't like the Byrons coming at all but I paid for them out of my money and that calmed down things a bit. Byron Stingily wasn't one to waste an opportunity so he suggested we stay an extra week and meet with some major labels. Byron called all the major labels, set up meetings and coordinated terms with DeWayne Powell in Chicago. We left there with major label deals for Ce Ce, Byron, Kym Mazelle, and a standing invitation for any other acts we brought.

It didn't start easy though. Our very first meeting was with Scott Folks. Scott had just woken up and made a comment that I thought was a joke, so I started laughing.

Scott gave me the meanest look ever and proceeded to tear into me and Byron for the next two hours about how unprofessional we were, how unprepared we were and we'd never get a deal because we didn't know what we were doing. We just sat there sweating bullets like we had a three digit fever. We couldn't say anything because he was right. I felt 2 inches tall again, but it was a bit better because when I looked over at Byron he seemed like he felt 1.5 inches tall. We were pretty traumatized by that and we wondered if it was even worth it staying in New York.

I put in an emergency call to my new girlfriend Miss Happy. I called her that because she was always cheerful, smiling, and with an unbelievably sensational body she made me happy too damnit. Byron and I shared the hotel room so we had to wait in the other bed until Byron fell asleep before Miss Happy could start cheering me up. I found out the next day that Byron hadn't actually fallen asleep yet, which was very embarrassing but I felt a lot better anyway.

The days meeting was with Merlin Bobb from Atlantic Records, and it was the greatest meeting ever. Merlin loved everything we played and was ready to sign whatever we had. Byron basically had carte blanche and Atlantic would sign him to any deal he wanted, with whatever act he wanted. He chose his friends Byron Burke and Herb Lawson. I named the group Ten City, short for intensity. I would have preferred a solo deal, because we were brothers and splitting everything 50/50, and when he added his boys that changed to a 25 percent split. I asked him why and he told me that he always wanted to be part of a group. Fair enough. Byron was very shy in the beginning. I remember maybe his first ten shows he performed with his eyes closed. So maybe the group idea was a good thing. Byron also came up with an awesome concept for Ten City where everything was peaceful and everyone lived in harmony.

Shortly after that Byron and I were on a double date with Gee Gee and Cynthia,(sorry Miss Happy!) I scored with Gee Gee because I had a hit record out but Byron was having a little trouble with Cynthia partly due to his shyness and he starting humming something so I joined in with some harmony humming and in the middle of the date we came up with the song *Devotion*. Merlin signed it immediately and release date was a month away.

Now Byron was a shy guy but he had a date and asked me for advice. He was a boob man like me and his date Sandra had an extra portion. She also invited him to her house for dinner.

Uh oh.

I told him one thing; do not eat anything red your first time over a woman's house.

Laugh if you want but word is some women (not saying SHE did it!) have been known to put period blood in food. This is meant to hook the man for life and guarantee a marriage. I've actually had women try it on me (more on that later) and while I don't personally believe it works, I don't *really* want that kind of seasoning in my food.

On the real tip I've seen guys hopelessly fall in love two notable times instantly and both said they had something red when they went over the woman's house on the first date.

So what happens? Byron calls me from over her house and reports that she's about to serve him spaghetti! "Don't eat it B!" Go hungry, I'll buy you some McDonalds later!"

He ate the spaghetti. As I said before, I don't really believe that stuff but a week later he calls me up and tells me he's getting married. I pleaded with him to just wait until his record came out and he could get all the women he wanted, but he wanted her. Aw man, I can't talk anyone out of shit. He did have a wonderful family though so it worked out great, but he was so shy I would've just liked to see how he handled all the attention from females if he was single, what a shame. Byron was notable throughout the music industry for never cheating on his wife, everyone treated him like he was a unicorn, they couldn't believe it.

CHAPTER SEVEN

In my opinion Marshall is a legend and has been such an important part of the creation of House music from the very start. House music just wouldn't be the same without him. He has produced so many hit records from the early days, for himself, other artists and also under different aliases like Virgo and Jungle Wonz for example. The tracks he made under those names define the House sound perfectly for me, a bit of Chicago magic, and they are still personal favourites of mine. I remember in 86 when House started making a rumble in the UK – very exciting times. The music was sounding new and fresh and there were so many great new tracks hitting our shores. Then I heard Move Your Body *for the first time and was blown away by the energy of this track and the epic piano hook, complimented by the vocals of Curtis Mclain. It was labelled* The House Music Anthem, *and rightly so, it still gets the clubs rocking when it drops nowadays. Another massive favourite of mine is* Open Our Eyes *by Marshall, an ambient masterpiece and an absolute classic sealed in history.*

I was lucky enough to play alongside Marshall recently. I never imagined, after first hearing Marshall's music all those years ago, that I would share a stage with him all these years later. It was a defining moment in my DJ career.

Nicky Brown (Centreforce Radio)

So in 1987 I produced Ce Ce Rogers, Ten City, and Kym Mazelle, then did a European House tour. when I came to the UK for the First House Music Tour of Europe. This was in the early part of the year. I travelled there with a crew that included Adonis, Kevin Irving (who was going under the name Jackin' House at that time), Curtis McClain, Rudy Forbes, Robert Owens, Danny Wilson (who puts records out under other names and had also been a member of Full House who released *Communicate*) and Larry Heard. On the tour Frankie Knuckles had top billing but he wasn't on the tour.

Our first booking was at the Hippodrome in London. It was a huge venue that held over a thousand people just when they were seated. But on the night we played there it was pretty much empty. I don't know why. Maybe it there hadn't been enough promotion for the event or maybe it was just a matter of London not having that many people into House music around that time.

The most memorable part of the night happened when we couldn't find Kevin Irving anywhere. We searched all around the venue and were starting to get worried. But then we decided to try the front area of the venue and there he was. We found him having sex with some girl on the *front* stairs of the club, where anybody could see. The girl's name was Jackie and she had a friend called Joy. They ended up hanging out with us for the remainder of the tour.

After a disappointing London show we moved onto our next booking which was in a club called The Wall. I can't remember where that was but it was up North somewhere. That was also a huge club and that had a much better turn out; but still was not packed.

The third club that we went to was the Hacienda in Manchester. That was packed, the people were into it, they knew all the songs, and I pulled a beautiful girl named Teresa, who looked like Robin Givens and knew because she was told it constantly, so she was also ashamed of it. The DJ at the Hacienda was Mike Pickering. When I heard him play I thought he sounded just like a Chicago DJ. When he played *Give Me Back The Love* by On The House I was pretty much done, we had a British Househead. A few years later he did a cover of the Ce Ce Rogers' track *Someday* with his outfit M. People.

I must have played at the Hacienda at least twenty times and I have played at many events organised by the Hacienda people. Every time I play at the Hacienda people are always really into the music.

I don't recall exactly how many dates we played in the UK on that tour, but I do remember that we went to Rock City in Nottingham and for me that was the best night on the tour. It was a proper stage with professional spotlights, fog machines, and great live sound. The people there also knew every song, and screamed when the heard the first notes of each.

When I was back in London I finally got to meet up with Jazzy M too. I remembered how during those long telephone conversations with Jazzy M he'd tell me about kebabs and how, when I was in London, I should get myself one. When I visited Jazzy at his record shop which was called the Vinyl Zone he had a kebab shop next to it and I went in and I bought my first kebab. I ended buying a kebab every day after that. I can even remember staying at some hotel which was miles away from that kebab shop, but I jumped on the Tube just so that I get one.

While I was in London I was taken to a few clubs. The Wag on Wardour Street was an experience. Man, Derrick Boland played just about the greatest set I'd ever heard because he seamlessly mixed all genres on one dance floor, it was artistry man. Another club was called Heaven, which I went to about four times. Spectrum at Heaven was being run by Paul Oakenfold. He had been to Ibiza with Danny Rampling, Trevor Fung and Nicky Holloway and they'd been very impressed by what was happening on the island.

And I also went to Shoom which was a club in a fitness gym in Southwark being run by Danny Rampling. I believe that, like Oakenfold, after visiting Ibiza he too wanted to emulate that vibe back in London. I had hired a publicist named Patrick Lilly and it was him who told me about the club which he called the 'happy happy Shoom'. Well, Shoom was happy because of Danny Rampling, because he tore some shit up. He had hands in the air and screaming all night like a black country church.

When I was in the studio with Ten City, Peter and Joe Smooth would often drop by to see what I was doing and how I was doing it. Not long after Joe came out with *Promised*

Land, which was a song that sounded a lot like the stuff that I was doing around that time.

Promised Land was first issued on DJ International in 1987 and everybody loved it. The song was covered by The Style Council in 1989 and it was a top forty hit for them. Joe released *Promised Land* for a second time and it peaked around the fifties.

Joe and I became friends and have remained friends. He has always been a very pleasant guy. He's very soft spoken and I believe people find him easy to get along with.

Joe was known for playing the Smart Bar, which was a club that went off in the basement of an established music venue in Chicago called the Cabaret Metro. Bands liked New Order, The Bangles and Depeche Mode played in the place.

Cabaret Metro had been opened in the early 80s by Joe Shanahan. He had been inspired to open his own place after witnessing what was happening in the New York music scene. I think The Ramones were one of the first bands to perform in the place.

Another band to play at the venue was Cabaret Voltaire and it's said that Joe named his venue after the band, which is funny really because the band named themselves after a club in Switzerland called Cabaret Voltaire. It wasn't due to Joe or his venue, but I ended up producing and working with Cabaret Voltaire. They were flown out to Chicago so that we could get into the studio.

Cabaret Voltaire was made up of three guys: Richard H. Kirk, Stephen Mallinder and Chris Watson. They were from Sheffield in the UK and in the early 80s had built up a strong indie following after their albums *The Voice Of America* and *2X45*.

While they were in Chicago I took them to Cabaret Metro and Joe was really pleased about meeting them. He was really pleased that I was working with them, too.

I had been introduced to Cabaret Voltaire during my visit to the UK in 1987. I had flown over with DeWayne Powell, Ce Ce Rogers and Kym Mazelle. There was a meeting with the Cabaret Voltaire's manager and he asked me if I would produce the band's next record and I agreed. I also met ABC during that visit. I really loved ABC's music and at that time they were a hot dance act.

While Cabaret Voltaire was in Chicago I worked on three songs with them. One of the songs we did was called *Hypnotised* and they made a video to promote the track that was filmed around Chicago.

The reason why they came to Chicago rather than me go to the UK was because I had a fear of flying. I still do. I hate it but I have to do it. In the late 80s I had so much work on and money being thrown at me that I would refuse to fly anywhere, so if people wanted to work with me they had to come to wherever I was.

So Cabaret Voltaire flew out to Chicago and we worked together for about a month. During that month they went out partying every single night. They were kings of the city because all the alternative kids loved their music and they wanted to party with them. In fact one people found out that the band were in town everybody wanted a piece of them. The band didn't mind – they got quite into it, especially because they had Sleezy D on hand to show them around.

I went out with them on the first few nights but once I saw what they were getting up to and taking, I thought, 'Oh, fuck that' and I just let them go and enjoy themselves.

I remember that after the studio, Tony who was our limousine driver would take everybody back the band's hotel. The band would tell us that they needed to go to their hotel rooms and get prepared for the night's activity. Tony, Sleezy and me would be waiting for hours but, when they came back down, they would all still be wearing exactly the same clothes that they'd been wearing all day.

This happened a few times and then after another day in the studio and going back to their hotel I decided to go up to their room with them and find out why they always took so long. Sure enough I discovered that they were up there snorting up white powder like vacuum cleaners.

On special occasions I did have to fly and one of these trips was when I came to the UK for the First House Music Tour of Europe. This was in the early part of the year. I travelled there with a crew that included Adonis, Kevin Irving (who was going under the name Jackin' House at that time), Curtis McClain, Rudy Forbes, Robert Owens, Danny Wilson (who puts records out under other names and had also been a member of Full House who released *Communicate*) and Larry Heard. On the tour Frankie Knuckles had the top billing spot and he wasn't even on the tour.

Our first booking was at the Hippodrome in London. It was a huge venue that held over a thousand people just when they were seated. But on the night we played there it was pretty much empty. I don't know why. Maybe it there hadn't been enough promotion for the event or maybe it was just a matter of London not having that many people into House music around that time.

The most memorable part of the night happened when we couldn't find Kevin Irving anywhere. We searched all around the venue and were starting to get worried. But then we decided to try the front area of the venue and there he was. We found him having sex with some girl on some stairs, where anybody could see. The girl's name was Jackie and she had a friend called Joyce. They ended up hanging out with us for the remainder of the tour.

After a disappointing London show we moved onto our next booking which was in a club called The Wall. I can't remember where that was but it was up North somewhere. That was also a huge club and that had a much better turn out; but still was not packed.

The third club that we went to was the Hacienda in Manchester. The venue was on the corner of Whitworth Street and had been a warehouse where yachts were built. In the early 80s a guy called Rob Gretton opened the place as a music venue and he got Tony Wilson involved. Tony owned Factory Records. Factory Records had New Order on the label and the band also became partners in the club. I think the club struggled for a few years when it just had indie kids gathering there to listen to Smiths songs, but then House music started to be played and that changed everything for the club.

We were very well received in the Hacienda and that was when we first started to feel like rock stars. Playing at that club was an amazing experience. The Hacienda crowd were really into us and they knew every song that we performed.

The DJ at the Hacienda was Mike Pickering. When I heard him play I thought he sounded just like the guys back home in Chicago. Mike and another DJ called Graeme Park had been hosting successful nights at the Hacienda called Nude and that was where House music in Manchester really took off. I didn't really get to speak to Mike much that night but a few years later he did a cover of the Ce Ce Rogers' track *Someday* with his outfit M. People.

During my career I must have played at the Hacienda twenty times and I have played at many events organised by the Hacienda people. Every time I play at the Hacienda people are always really into the music.

I don't recall exactly how many dates we played in the UK on that tour, but I do remember that we went to Rock City in Nottingham and for me that was the best night on the tour.

When I was back in London I finally got to meet up with Jazzy M too. I remembered how during those long telephone conversations with Jazzy M he'd tell me about kebabs and how, when I was in London, I should get myself one. When I visited Jazzy at his record shop which was called the Vinyl Zone he had a kebab shop next to it and I went in and I bought my first kebab. I ended buying a kebab every day after that. I can even remember staying at some hotel which was miles away from that kebab shop, but I jumped on the Tube just so that I get one.

While I was in London I was taken to a few clubs. The Wag in Wardour Street was good fun. Another club was called Heaven, which I went to about four times. Spectrum at Heaven was being run by Paul Oakenfold. He had been to Ibiza with Danny Rampling, Trevor Fung and Nicky Holloway and they'd been very impressed by what was happening on the island.

And I also went to Shoom which was a club in a fitness gym in Southwark being run by Danny Rampling. I believe that, like Oakenfold, after visiting Ibiza he too wanted to emulate that vibe back in London. I had hired a publicist named Patrick Lilly and it was him who told me about the club which he called the 'happy happy Shoom'. Danny was a hot DJ who really tore some shit up on the night that I went.

The same year that I first visited London Trax Records also released *Time Marches On*. I had recorded the song the previous year and they had just sat on it. *Time Marches On* was put out as Jungle Wonz product. Jungle Wonz was a project that I did with Harry Dennis. It was Harry that came up with the lyrics to *Time Marches On* and that had inspired me to come up with the music. I also sang on the song along with Harry 'You can live, you can die, there ain't no time to wonder why, life is short, life is long. We have a choice to live or die. Nothing stays the same. Time marches on.'

The song really was built around Harry's lyrics and it all came together very quickly. *Time Marches On* was one of those times in life when everything just comes together with little effort. It was meant to be.

It was me who came up with the name Jungle Wonz. This was partly inspired by the first song that Harry and me did called *The Jungle* and instead of writing 'ones' I thought a cooler spelling would be 'wonz'.

1987 was also important for me because that was the year that I got my first major record deals. This was after I had been to New York with Byron Stingily. We'd done I *Can't Stay Away* under the name Ragtyme by then. Byron and I worked on a few songs but it took us a while to discover his full potential. I mean, Byron is a big motherfucker and I knew he had the power, but I felt he wasn't using it. We had to work to find it and it was while we were in the studio recording *I Can't Stay Away* that we found it. At one point in the song he hit a high note and it was like 'there it is'. We found his power.

I first met Byron down at Trax Records. He was with another guy called Des and they had a group together. They dressed like Prince and looked like they came out of Minneapolis. Byron actually came from the West Side of Chicago, which was the rough part of town.

Byron and I hit it off right from the first moment. He was cool and he was humble. We started hanging out and would go on double dates and do stuff like that. Our friendship came first and making music came second. Byron really caught my vibe. When he listened to my music he really understood it. It was certain that we'd end up making music together. At the time Ten City didn't exist.

When On The House went to New York to do some shows Byron Stingily and Byron Burke came along too and in the middle of the set they would perform *I Can't Stay Away*. Curtis and Rudy weren't over the moon about that but we did it anyway. I just wanted to get Byron out in front of people.

Now Byron isn't one to miss an opportunity so it was his idea to stick around New York for a couple of weeks and go and meet up with some of the various major record labels around town.

Somehow Byron managed to get us in the door of several majors and by the end of the two weeks I had so many labels wanting a piece of me. Full credit to Byron on this because he really did pull it off.

The first meeting we had was with Capitol Records. Scott Volks. I remember walking into Scott's offices and noticing what looked like a cot. There was some sheets and stuff and it was obvious that they were being used. Not thinking too much about it I just blurted out 'Hey man, you sleeping in here?'

I couldn't have said a worse thing because he got really angry about it. He was really pissed off with me and for the next two hours all he seemed to do was insult Byron and me. He put us down for showing up at his office with no press pack and being underprepared for such a meeting. He really made us sweat and we just sat there and took it. We left his office like we had a three-digit fever and we never went back.

I saw Scott the following year at the New Music Seminar. By this time Ten City was doing well, Kym Mazelle was doing well and I was big news in the world of dance music. He actually approached me and wanted to talk and I reminded him about what he said regards my music not being able to do shit. He just kind of shuffled off. He ended up getting fired from Capitol and moved to a different label and he called me wanting to hear some of my music. We were all good after that.

Now that Byron and I had interest from major record labels we got to working on new songs. The label that we ended signing with was Atlantic Records. It was Merlin Bobb, the label's A&R man who signed us. Atlantic wanted something quick so that was when Ten City came about. The first song we wrote was *Devotion*.

Merlin was also a DJ and he played *Devotion* on his WBLS radio show. He was the biggest radio DJ on the East Coast at the time so when he played our record a lot of people got to hear it.

People went nuts over *Devotion* and it got sampled and covered loads of times. The first person to sample the song was Todd Terry on his Black Riot stuff. A few years after that Nomad covered it. Their version got to number two in the UK charts. To be honest I didn't really like their song. Not so much them, I just kinda look down on people that sample and lift stuff from other people I think it's the lazy way. I'm also an underground guy and, when something is too commercial, it takes something away for me.

Ten City was formed of Byron Stingily who sang, Byron who played keyboards and Herb Lawson who played guitar and I was the producer. I have this thing when I work with people and it's to do with how percentages work. For example if there are only two of us on the song we split the royalty 50/50. It doesn't matter how much work you did, that's the agreement. I mean if you just farted on the record you'd get your fifty percent. If there are four people involved then it's twenty-five per cent each.

Once the two Byrons, Herb and myself agreed on this we next had to come up with a group name. I offered up the name Intensity. They guys thought that that was okay but then Byron Stingily suggested rewording it to Ten City. Now Byron is one creative dude and he then came up with this whole concept about Ten City being a place where people can go and everybody would be free and dance and get along. We all agreed.

We spent 1988 recording the first Ten City album which was called *Foundation*. It took us quite a long time to finish the album because we were also touring a lot of the time too. I mean there was a lot of money being thrown at us for doing shows and we didn't want to turn any of that down. I was also getting pulled into other projects with people like Kym Mazelle and Ce Ce Rogers and I was taking trips to the UK again. It was an incredibly busy time for me.

Foundation did get finished though and it included songs like *Devotion, Right Back To You* and *That's The Way Love Is*. *That's The Way Love Is* was the song that really broke the band and it went to number one in the US dance charts. Steve 'Silk' Hurley was brought in to do a Deep House mix and people went crazy of it – they still are!

I have to admit that I didn't especially like *That's The Way Love Is* at first because Merlin Bobb did a remix of it and messed around with it too much for my liking. But once things like snare drums and another piano were added I grew to like the song. I though the piano was out of this world and when it breaks off into that piano solo at the end, oh boy!

The sleeve notes on *Foundation* provided Ten City with an opportunity to thank people and a lot of guys got name checked. The list included: Ron Hardy, Frankie Knuckles, Kiss FM, Fingers Inc, The Hot Mix 5, the crew at Black Market Records in London, Kym Mazelle and Ce Ce Rogers. These represented the people who were around us at that time. The guys also added a special message to me: To Marshall, the man with the plan, thanks for sharing our vision. You're a superstar, you're the greatest!

The other deal I had with Atlantic Records concerned Ce Ce Rogers and *Someday*. My connection to Ce Ce happened during my trip to New York. I hooked up with a guy called Billy who ran three clubs in the city: Club America, Club 88 and Zanzibar.

Billy gave us the first class treatment when we went to his clubs. Anything we wanted we were given. Anything we didn't want we were also given. And he had us driven around in a limo everywhere, too.

It was while hanging out with Billy that he passed me a tape. He told me there was a singer on there that he wanted me to listen to. I took the tape but put it away and didn't really think too much more on it. A few weeks later Billy contacted me and asked me if I had come up with a song for the singer on the tape yet.

I still hadn't listened to the tape but I told Billy I had a song called *Someday* that I had written and needed a vocalist for. The next thing I know Ce Ce is being flown into Chicago to see me.

We recorded *Someday* in the Streeterville Studios in Chicago. During one session Ce Ce started playing the keyboard and he was really good. The thing was Billy had specifically told him not to play the keyboard. Now Ce Ce was a Berkley Music Collage graduate and this meant that he was a musician extraordinaire. He was really up there. The reason Billy had told Ce Ce not to play anything was because he thought if I heard how good Ce Ce was it would fuck with my confidence. It was okay though and it didn't affect me at all and we pushed on and recorded *Someday*.

Just before Ce Ce was flown to Chicago I had sent Billy a tape with the song on it. On that version I was doing the singing. Billy passed the tape onto Ce Ce so that he could learn it. This meant that when Ce Ce got into the studio he was ready to go. I played the song and we recorded his vocals and he got it down perfect. In one take we had Ce Ce's amazing vocals. The girls that were in the studio with us were swooning. What he did was magical. Incredible! But Ce Ce, who was carrying all this Berkley music stuff, figured that he'd fucked up and he wanted to do his vocals again. He looked at me and says 'I want to do it again' to which I replied 'No man, we're done here'. But Ce Ce pleaded with me. He really felt that what he had done just wasn't good enough. I protested again but in the end surrendered and said to the studio engineer, 'Hey man let Ce Ce record his vocals as many times as he wants. You'll find me in McDonalds'.

Once Atlantic got stuck in Ce Ce then said he wanted to re-record his vocals again. We all rolled our eyes but let him get on and do it again. But you know what? After all those recordings, we wound up using the original that was first laid down.

We got there in the end and I like the song very much. I particularly like the piano on it. I played that piano and it fitted so well with Ce Ce's wonderful vocals. I think of his vocals as being over worldly.

Someday was later sampled by Liquid for their song *Sweet Harmony* and M. People covered it too. In 1996 *Mixmag* placed the song at number three as their 100 Greatest Dance Singles of All Time.

CHAPTER EIGHT

Marshall 'so much more than just Move Your Body'
Jefferson, he had quite a few aliases too. While some get called
House music pioneers, Marshall truly was a pioneer, after all,
it did all start in Chicago. Sixty next year, he continues to rock.
Graham Gold

As 1988 rolled on it came to my attention that the British kids
were really getting into House music in a big way. It had been
small and to some extent contained by a few people that were
really into it. I think some of them wanted to keep the music
and their scene a secret.

I would hear about guys like Boys Own, which was Terry
Farley and Andrew Weatherall and Genesis, which was
Wayne Anthony and you had Andy Swallow who in 1989
would found the pirate radio station Centreforce, all putting on
parties in warehouses and fields in the countryside outside of
London. At first the numbers who attended were small, just a
few hundred; but in a short space of time those numbers would
swell into the thousands. And they were all illegal parties that
just played House music.

People started to call what was happening in 1988 the Second Summer of Love. Acid House was all the rage. Kids danced around in smiley face T-shirts and dropped acid and ecstasy and had the night of their lives. By the summer of 89 people were calling the parties raves and there were organisations like Sunrise, Biology and Energy putting on huge raves in warehouses and fields and there'd be like fairground rides and spectacular laser shows.

When I was in England in the summer of 88 I was taken to one of these illegal parties. I had been playing somewhere and straight after I finished I was ushered into a car and driven off into the countryside. I have no idea where I was taken. What I recall is that it was pitch black. We got to this place and the music playing but I couldn't see shit. It was that dark I was stepping on people. It was all a bit too much for me and I didn't connect with it. This wasn't like anything I had ever seen back in Chicago. I mean, a party in some countryside ass field? Fuck no!

The people I was with led me to where the DJs were and asked if I wanted to play. I declined. I then asked when the lights would be coming on, but was told that there wouldn't be any lights because it was an illegal party. 'Illegal party?' I said, 'fuck this shit, take me back to my hotel'. I couldn't afford to get arrested in England, for fuck's sake. I didn't know what the situation was at all. All I knew was that I needed to get out of there.

Alongside the US House music the UK acid house scene was also being fuelled by music being made by guys from the UK. Among them there was 808 State and A Guy Called

Gerald. They all came out of Manchester. A Guy Called Gerald put out *Voodoo Ray* and that was a massive song for the acid house parties. I thought it was a nice song. It just felt that it was a long way behind what we'd been doing in Chicago a few years earlier. At first I didn't even know that *Voodoo Ray* was a UK song. I thought it had been done by one of the guys in Chicago. So I guess credit to Gerald for that.

Before acts from Manchester like 808 State, A Guy Called Gerald and groups like the Stone Roses and the Happy Mondays were getting popular, the city had New Order. They had been making songs for several years before acid house kicked off in the Hacienda. They were involved with the Hacienda Club. I love *Blue Monday*. I think that's a great song. They had another song called *Confusion* that I really liked too. That was very electro-sounding. I believe the band had gone to New York soon after they formed and while there visited some of the clubs and what they heard inspired their sound.

Coming out of the south of England there was also people making House music. One of the more successful from that late 80s period was Adamski. He captured the essence of the raves from that time. He had a big hit with Seal which was called *Killer*. That was a song that I liked a lot. I didn't think of it as being a House record though.

As the years have passed I have played with the guys from 808 State and Gerald Simpson on several occasions. Gerald is a very nice guy. I think I lives in Germany now but the 808 State guys are still in the Manchester area.

Some people also called 1989 the Second Summer of Love. I worked a lot during that year. Ten City took up a lot of my time. The year climaxed when Ten City performed on New Year's Eve at the Fridge in Brixton. Kym Mazelle also performed that night. It was a high point of the year. I remember the guy who introduced Ten City onto stage telling people that *Foundation* was the album of the future and the crowd got really excited. I remember feeling the excitement building in the room as twelve o'clock approached and then the sound system went down. Silence!

Life got very busy for me and I had to juggle my work with Ten City along with other people. Because of this the second album which was called *State of Mind* also got delayed coming out. During this time I also changed my managers and I went from being with DeWayne Powell to Craig Kallman.

Craig owned his own label called Big Beat Records. When I met Craig he was fresh out of college and a good-looking Jewish kid. He worked hard to build up his label and he'd call me up, always beginning with 'Maaarrrssshhhaaalll'. He was so funny. Craig really pushed to get one of my songs out on Big Beat.

Craig had started out as a DJ in various clubs around New York and he kept all that going while he was at college. He was a guy who'd make things happen and get things done. I remember that he when he was still a college kid he had a video made and somehow he managed to get a bunch of Hollywood A-listers feature in it. I was impressed when I heard about his video and we started to hang out and listen to rock and roll music. He had a huge record collection. I mean, he had a loft that was jam-packed full of records.

I got talking to Craig about the record deal that I had secured for Ten City at Atlantic, which I think was eighty thousand dollars. Eighty thousand dollars is a lot of money but Craig told me that was a price that was right at the bottom of what major record labels paid for new groups. I didn't know anything about these bargain basement deals. At the time I just wanted a record deal with a major label and to have records put out.

Craig and I also got talking about the promotion that the labels do and it was clear to me that Atlantic hadn't really pushed the Ten City album much at all. Atlantic kind of relied on people buying *Foundation* because they knew that it was Marshall Jefferson that had produced the album.

Both the debut albums for Ten City and Ce Ce Rogers went Gold and what I did learn was that Atlantic Records Black Music Department made their first profit with the Ten City and Ce Ce Rogers records since 1967 and that was back in the days of Aretha Franklin. I know now that the success of my music from that time paid for a lot of Atlantic acts that followed the Ten City and Ce Ce stuff.

It was while I was in Craig's loft listening to rock music and talking one day that Craig convinced me to leave DeWayne Powell and allow him to manage me. He said he could promote my music and get better deals for me. I had to think about it, but I went with him.

One of our first meetings was with MCA Records. The guy there wanted me to produce a new act he had who was called Chris Sutton. During the meeting Craig stepped in and told the guy that if he wanted me to produce his act there would be a seventy-five thousand dollar price tag. I couldn't believe my ears. I had no idea that Craig was going ask for anything near that. But Craig didn't just stop there. He continued by telling the guy that the deal would also need to include this and that too. I mean, Craig had a list.

Craig secured that deal and I had this artist called Chris Sutton to produce. It was because I was now into the Sutton album that the follow-up Ten City took a while. This caused a lot of tension between me and the Ten City guys. They couldn't move forward without me and I was too busy getting pulled in other directions.

Now getting back to Chris Sutton, that was an experience in itself. The album we made never even came out. Chris had a very strong personality. He was a very good looking guy who reminded me of a young Peter Frampton. He was from somewhere in the UK and he was writing House and pop songs. He was also a fantastic singer.

We wrote two songs together and we're ready to go into the studio to record them. But in the studio he wanted to produce his own vocals his own way. The way he wanted to do it was to sing a small section, sometimes just a few words and then stop. His intention was to sing every note fucking perfect. That was not my way of working at all.

I don't know how many overdubs we ended up doing but it took us fourteen hours. By the time we started working on the second song I had some idea how to produce his vocals and what he would need.

We had a Synclavier keyboard in the studio. That was an early digital synthesizer and sampling system. It cost a fortune.

The Synclavier had a module on it where you pitch the vocals and move into a certain place. This meant the end result could be a perfect pitch vocal. Why the fuck did I show Chris that? By the third song that we worked on we had two studios running and that was just to pitch his vocals.

It was painful playing back the songs that we did because Chris would always point out something that he didn't like or that he didn't think was right. But there's was nothing wrong and his vocals were totally fine.

Chris and I would never do less than twelve-hour sessions in the studio and this went on for two months. He was a bit of taskmaster in the studio too and if I or anyone else in the studio got a phone call he would give you such a glare. For Chris, being in the studio meant work. For me, being in the studio meant fun.

But as good as the album was it just never got released. This was partly due to the guy from the label we had been dealing with originally leaving the label. The new guy moved in and just didn't get involved with what we had been doing. I guess he had his own projects to push and move forward.

The other project that distracted me from the second Ten City album was to do an album with a female artist called Vicky Ryan. Vicky was a stripper from New Jersey. She was a beautiful woman. It was because of her boyfriend Troy that I got involved with her. Troy suggested I should work with Vicky but I was reluctant. All I knew was that she was a stripper. I didn't know if she could sing. But Troy convinced me and she was flown into Chicago.

We wrote a song called *Mister Groove*. *Mister Groove* was a twenty-minute-long song. It had similarities to *Love to Love You Baby* by Donna Summer. There were some high points working on that song. One was getting the Chicago Symphony Orchestra in to play on it.

We played the song to Craig and he went off with the tape. Soon after he got back to us and he'd secured us a record deal with SBK Records. During this time SBK Records signed Vanilla Ice, Technotronic and Boy George and a big act for them in the 90s was Blur.

The deal he managed to secure for Vicky had the highest royalty rate in the history of music. Craig also managed to put a clause in the contract that said that if anyone on the label got a higher royalty rate than Vicky, then hers had to be raised to match it. Her deal also had advances, tour support and guaranteed promotion. Craig really did secure her a big fucking deal.

At the time of doing the album the A&R guy that we had been dealing with closed a few deals with other acts that all blew up and got very successful. As a result SBK moved him to New York and gave him a massive promotion. I mean, he was their golden boy.

Now, for some reason that guy had second thoughts about releasing the Viki album. I don't know why. I do remember his high-maintenance girlfriend though, who would scream up at him in front of everybody. It was embarrassing to watch.

That guy was only twenty-two years old too and all of a sudden he has all this success and a big promotion. I think there were some people at the SBK who just didn't appreciate this younger man becoming their boss. I think they didn't help him and would even feed him the wrong information and this somehow connected to the Viki album and, long story short, her album wasn't released. I think the label had issues and they lost some of their artists. I think Vanilla Ice was among them and that was foolish of them to lose him because after *Ice Ice Baby* he could have released a fart and it would have gone platinum.

Craig Kallman was a good guy and he and I worked together for some time. He actually ended up selling Big Beat to Atlantic Records in 1991 and shortly after became vice president of Atlantic.

After working with Chris Sutton and Vicky Ryan I eventually got into a space where I could resume my relationship with Ten City. All the time I had been working on other projects although the guys couldn't record they because were still out there touring. While they were on the road they also started to write new songs. The one member I saw often during that time was 'Guitar' Herb and this was because I had brought him in to play guitar on the Sutton and Ryan albums. Herb was my default guitarist. I would pay him fifteen hundred to two thousand dollars per song. The labels would also complain to me about that but I would say, 'This is Guitar Herb from Ten City; you better give him two grand before he asks for four'.

When it came time to discuss what deal was being offered Craig, who was managing me, went to have the talks. He basically told Atlantic that I wanted 75, 000 dollars. Atlantic wasn't happy about that because the budget they were offering to pay for the entire album was only eighty thousand dollars. But Craig dug in and told Atlantic that I was worth double that.

Following Atlantic's meeting with Craig they then went and had meetings with the Ten City guys. They told them that Marshall Jefferson was asking for more money than all of them put together. Understandably that pissed them off and Byron called me up. We talked and I said they should ask for more money too because that was Atlantic Records and they have plenty of money. I reminded Byron that Ten City's debut album went gold and I that if Atlantic treated the group properly the second album could go platinum.

Unfortunately the Ten City guys just thought I was being greedy and asking for too much money and that they wouldn't get a fair share. In the end I negotiated with them and I wound up doing *State of Mind* for twenty thousand dollars. The thing was I didn't write any of the songs of that album. They had been writing while they had been on the road. I felt there was some hostility coming from the guys towards me during the making of that album, but in time we straightened it all out.

It felt like Ten City was on a non-stop tour from late 1987 to 1990. Alongside the UK we also went to other places in Europe. I had first visited some of those places on the first House tour back in 87. Italy and Germany was included on those trips. Our music was very well received there. I remember in Germany the Berlin Wall was still up so we didn't go into East Germany. I did get to venture into that part of the country a few years later and pretty soon after the Wall had been knocked down. I remember noticing sections of the Wall still standing. I guess it was left there to remind people of those days when there was a divide. Or maybe they just hadn't got around to demolishing those parts.

When I was able to travel all over Germany techno was the sound that had really become massive. There were several guys out there who made that music but they made it their own and it sounded nothing like the Detroit sound or the New York sound.

Todd Terry is a good friend. He was part of that New York scene. They were making their own House music. It sounded like it could have come out of Chicago but they called it techno.

The first time I heard anything about Todd was when Little Louie Vega (one of the guys from Masters at Work) gave me a tape with Todd on it. He told me that he was playing the stuff at his club which at that time was called Heartthrob. Louie was a guy from the Bronx in New York and put parties on all around the Bronx and Manhattan area in the 80s. On that tape was a remix of *Move Your Body* which was *Can U Party*. Todd was going under the name Royal House at that time.

I wasn't that thrilled about somebody remixing *Move Your Body* and the reason was that I didn't want to make Larry Sherman any more money. I guess I knew if monies made from Todd's record would find its way back to Trax Records and I was unlikely to see any of it.

I listened to the tape that Louie had given me but didn't really think too much about it. I forgot about it until I heard it again once it had been released. There was my song all chopped up in a new song called *Can U Party*. I thought it was a pretty hot song.

It was Todd who really made sampling a big thing. Personally I don't sample other people's records. There's a part of me that's always viewed sampling as cheating and the easy way to make a song. It does kind of bother me when I hear somebody sample one of my songs. I couldn't sample someone else's song then call it my own. It just wouldn't feel right to me.

I first met Todd in London in the late 80s. We had both been booked to play at the same show. Ten City and Kym Mazelle were also on the bill. Back then Todd was very shy. When we were introduced you could see that he felt quite intimidated to meet me. We didn't really speak much. Maybe I had given him one of my 'Yeah, I know what you did' looks. Nowadays Todd is pretty loud and confident and he is well respected in the music industry. We still end up playing at the same places and it's always good to see him.

Before New York was doing their thing there was Derrick May, Kevin Saunderson, Juan Atkins in Detroit. Those guys were from the Belleville area of Detroit and became known as the Belleville Three. What those guys done laid the blueprint for what New York did and then what the German guys did.

In some ways techno kinda stopped in the US after Kevin and Derrick moved on to do other things. It wasn't like House music where there were lots of guys making House music. I mean the techno that exists today has little connection to what those early guys did in Detroit and New York. Kevin was part of Inner City who was also from Detroit and they had huge hits with *Big Fun* and *Good Life*.

I like a lot of that German techno. One guy I especially like is Cosmic Baby. His name is Harald Bluchel and he'd grown up in Germany listening to Kraftwerk and then he got into making House music and then techno. He later went on to form Energy 52 who put out *Café Del Mar*; which was a big Ibiza track. Yeah I loved the Cosmic Baby stuff. He made some beautiful songs.

Ibiza has helped boost the careers of many DJs and producers over the years. I have played there around thirty times. Although House music had been played in Ibiza since the mid 80s and people were putting on House parties all over the island since the late 80s, I didn't get out there until 1993. By then the scene was thriving.

I played at a party at Manumission which means 'release from slavery' and the idea that people were free to do whatever they wanted – and they did. Another place I liked to play was the Ku Club. Now Ku is supposed to be the largest club in the world. It has a capacity of 10,000 people. Whenever I played there it felt like there were a lot more than that in there.

Ibiza was party land. The hippies started going there in the 60s and then throughout the 70s people would go there to party. By the 80s it was a Mecca for people into acid house music and several clubs catered for their needs.

There was a DJ called Alfredo that was very instrumental in giving birth to the House music scene in Ibiza. Alfredo Fiorito was from Argentina but had gone to live in Ibiza in the 70s. Amnesia, near San Rafael was the club that he deejayed at and where guys like Danny Rampling and Paul Oakenfold first heard him.

I met Alfredo. At first I thought he was quite old-looking and not anything like the other guys around at the time. He was very soft spoken. I found him to be very friendly and a pleasure to be around. He's became known as the 'Father of the Balearic Beat'. To be honest before I went to Ibiza I really didn't know too much about him. But what I did know was that everybody from the UK held him in high regard, so I guess whatever he was doing had had a huge impact on the British House music culture.

I have never really explored Ibiza. I hear it has beautiful beaches and places to hang out but, by the time I was going out to the island, I was already a one day in and one day out guy; so I never really experience much of the places where I go.

The way I conduct my business now has a lot to do with getting high. Back in the days when I was getting high I would want to party all night long and way into the next day. It was easy for me to go from party to party to party. But I stopped in 1986. Since 1986 I haven't taken any drugs, drank any alcohol or even smoked a cigarette.

The thing was that when I was playing out and having songs being released like *Move Your Body*, everywhere I went I had people offering me this drug or that drug. People just wanted to offer me free shit: weed, coke, pills, drink. But I knew that if I went down that road I would become a casualty. You see, I'm the sort of guy who when he gets into it, he is really into it. When I'm doing something I'm really doing it and throw everything into it. I can be intense like that and I told myself that, if I continue to take all this free shit off of people, I might not live that long. So I stopped everything because I didn't want to end like Jimi Hendrix.

For people in the music business it can be a tough environment to be. Not all are able to place a limitation on what they do or who they are around and sadly there have been many casualties.

I actually found it quite easy to give up the drugs and drink. Once I had my mind up and told myself I was done with it, I just stopped. There was no gradual process, I just stopped. And hey, I'm still alive.

Not taking drugs and not being drunk has helped give me a clear perception of what goes on in front of me. When I'm in the DJ booth I see things. In the late 80s when acid house and rave was happening everybody in the clubs was on acid or ecstasy. It didn't bother me at all. I accepted it as being part of the clubbing culture. I knew how they were feeling because I had used the drugs that they had taken.

The music I made was for high people. I was fully aware of that. I understood that someone on acid or ecstasy could engage with songs like *Time Marches On*, *The Jungle* or *Move Your Body*.

When I'm in the DJ booth and people come up to me I can tell what drug they have done. I can tell by the way they're acting. I know when someone is on a dry high or a wet high. A dry high is when someone is on something like ecstasy and a wet high is when someone is drinking. The only time I find it annoying is when someone's breath stinks. When someone's been drinking and they're getting right up in your face what I'm thinking is, 'God damn, get the fuck out of here'.

By and large I just accept people and whatever they're doing. It's never really been an issue for me. I certainly understand that it's part of the scene and people have the choice to do whatever they want. People just want to go out and have a good time.

Over the years I have seen friends and other DJs go up and down with drugs and alcohol. It got the better of Ron Hardy. But most manage okay. I've seen many A-list superstars getting high. Drugs and alcohol are always around in the industry.

I remember being on one of the panels of the New Music seminars with Tony Wilson from Factory Records. Before the event started we were all in hanging around in the backstage area. I was just sitting quietly on a chair. I hadn't met Tony before. I just knew that he was pushing the live music acts from Manchester at the time like the Stone Roses and the Happy Mondays and of course the Hacienda. Tony walked into the room with his entourage and dumped a gigantic bag of coke onto the table. Now everybody in the room dived into that bag and started to hoover up. Tony invited me to partake but I declined just saying, 'No man, I'm good'.

Myself and the other guys on that panel with Tony Wilson were there to discuss a topic about America not respecting its own artists. There was talk about when the Beatles came to the States and being a huge success but the artists that the Beatles had drawn inspiration from were now washing dishes and being bus boys. Now, Derrick May was one of the other guys on the panel. Derrick is one of the funniest guys you'll ever meet and he can also be very outspoken. For some reason he had been running late so he hadn't been hanging out backstage with us in the ready room. This meant that he didn't really know what the topic was and when Tony was talking Derrick pipes up and says, 'Hey man, what the fuck are you talking about? I ain't washing no dishes. I'm making more money than you'. Tony and Derrick and the other guys on the panel then started to get into some argument and I said 'Oh fuck this' and I walked off of the panel and went home.

As the 80s went into the 90s and dance music changed, and all these new genres sprang up, the choice of drugs also started to change. Where it had been acid and ecstasy and weed the acid seemed to disappear and the quality of pills got worse. People started to take more pills on their nights out 'double drop'. And then cocaine became really popular. Ever since the 70s and through the 80s coke had always been there, but it was an expensive drug and not everyone could afford it. By the early 90s the price came down so kids were able to purchase wraps with grams of coke in it.

Some people say that with the introduction of coke the clubbing scene changed and people didn't dance as much. I didn't really notice that. All I saw was a lot of kids screaming away and putting their hands in the air when I played. As long as people didn't invade my personal space I didn't think too much about what sort of high they were on.

I had plenty of work on and was travelling the world and meeting all sorts of people. I would play my set and then leave. But just like everybody else I needed something to wind down with. For me it was video games.

I have played video games with so many people. Some of my most memorable times have been with the boys from Detroit: Derrick May, Kevin Saunderson and Mike 'Hitman' Wilson, who did *Can You Jack* with Bad Boy Bill (real name William Renkosik) and Bam Bam, whose real name is Chris

Westbrook. Bam Bam would fire everybody up and talk so much shit, because he would lose every time. We had great times sitting around playing Nintendo games like Double Dribble.

Playing video games has stuck with me for all these years. Actually *Move Your Body* was used in Grand Theft Auto San Andreas. I also heard that *Someday* that I did with Ce Ce Rogers and *Devotion* that I did with Ten City were also used in games too.

Getting a song in a video game can be a good earner but the manager I had at the time did a deal where he basically sold the songs for one-off deals of somewhere between ten and fifteen thousand dollars per song. Playing video games remain a constant in my life and it certainly helps make life on the road more tolerable.

CHAPTER NINE

Marshall Jefferson is one of our maestros. Since the early beginning of House music in the 80s, he was there composing and releasing the deepest tunes. Every time that we were selecting twelve-inches in the various records shops in Milano or somewhere else, we were choosing immediately all wax mentioning his name in the label copy. Then we were moving to our studio to put the needle on the records and study his natural way to give us emotions through his enchanted melodies with the deepest chords on each release. When we met him personally we were touched by his modesty and sincerity. Marshall Jefferson is the "Godfather" of House Music and for us is a living legend.
Harley & Muscle

My career has taken many diversions and because of my work I got contacted by all sorts of people asking me to get involved with them. The Tom Tom Club had nothing to do with House music but those guys liked what I did. I went to a studio in New York for that particular project. Unique Recording Studios had been booked. That was a very influential studio for hip hop located near Times Square. Lots of hip hop artists had recorded there: LL Cool J, Public Enemy, Run DMC.

Tom Tom Club was Chris Frantz and Tina Weymouth. They were also members of Talking Heads, who were part of the New York punk CBGB's scene and had hits with songs like *Psycho Killer* and *Burning Down the House*.

I spoke to Chris on the phone and was told that he wanted me to do some remixes on his music. I never got to meet Chris or Tina. We just talked over the phone and they wished me luck and gave me full autonomy to work on the remixes. The song I worked on was called *Suboceana* which was a song that Chris and Tina included on their album called *Boom Boom Chi Boom Boom*. I did two remixes of the song that got released as a twelve-inch. I wanted to do a club speed mix and the other at a more mid tempo. I got in Herb Lawson from Ten City too to add a guitar solo. I believe *Suboceana* got some attention in the clubs in the UK.

Although I got a lot of work from artists in the US I was also getting offers from the UK too. Around 1989 Duran Duran approached me to work with them. They had been recording an album called *Big Thing* which was something like their fifth or sixth album. They had been a group for more than a decade and had been hugely successful as New Romantic pop group.

We all got together in a studio and I recorded them live. It was very involved because alongside the main band members there was a horn section too. Despite working on the song called *Drug (It's a State of Mind)* I didn't actually finish that project, it just never got to the final mix stage. A version of the song mixed by Daniel Abraham was later released.

Duran Duran actually came to Los Angeles for that recording. The Sunset Sound Recording Studios were hired. This was where Led Zeppelin, The Doors and the Rolling Stones had recorded so it was a very professional studio with an incredible history. I found working with the Duran Duran guys interesting, but I don't want to say too much about that.

I remember that being in LA was a bit of a party. Once Dwayne Powell had set up the work we decided to make a week of it and we arranged to meet up with Oprah Winfrey and her hairstylist Andre. They were living the high life and were being driven around in Rolls Royces – it was first class all the way for them. I had a Californian girlfriend at the time so I introduced her to Duran Duran and of course Andre did her hair.

Going into 1990 I was just so busy and I was involved with so many projects, but being so busy I found that I just wasn't always able to totally focus and give each project the care that they deserved.

I did Marshall Jefferson Presents Umosia *We Are Unity (Strip It Down)*. This came about after Roy Davis Jr and Leonard Juniel came to see me. They brought a tape which we played in my basement. I put the tape on and after about fifteen seconds I stopped the tape, looked up at Roy and Leonard, grinned and said 'Hey that's really good, let's go'. We did the track and that was the start of Roy's career. We got in a female vocalist called Sheena Mahone to sing on the track and she was an excellent singer. Roy, Leonard and Sheena were all Chicago people.

We Are Unity (Strip It Down) was issued on Other Side Records. This was my record label that I started up and ran out of Chicago. The label had started back in 1985 with the Virgo Go Wild Rhythm Trax but going into the 90s I wanted to run it properly. The label's name Other Side was inspired by the name of a club in Chicago that was called Other Side.

During the label's life I put out records like *Music* by Reggie Hall, *Missing You* by Eleven, *Space Track* by Bam Bam and *The Way I Feel* by Musical Expression. I wrote and produced a lot of the stuff that came out on Other Side.

In 1994 I released a compilation album called *This Is Other Side Records* and that included tracks by Vicki Ryan, Party Girls, Two Meanings and Bigger Than Life. The Chicago Symphony Orchestra played on every track. Two Meanings was me, just me. I did two instrumentals under that name. The one I included on the compilation album was *My Life to Live*. I cannot recall where the name Two Meanings came from but I guess I thought it sounded kinda heavy at that time. I was living in Calumet City around that time. I had a place there for a while. Bigger Than Life was Chauncey Alexander's group. They had the songs *High and Mighty* and *All For Love* and I produced them. Musical Expression was three girls: Barbaria, Michelle and Trudie (RIP) and Chauncey worked with them too. They had a very good track with *The Way I Feel*. At first I called them Attitude but we discovered that there was another group with that name so we had to come up with an alternative name quickly. Barbaria, Michelle and

Trudie came to my attention after I held auditions for the 'diva'-style group that we wanted for Other Side Records.

Vicki Ryan, who was the exotic dancer that I have mentioned, had her song *Mister Groove* included on the album too. It was the long version coming in at twenty-three minutes. The music was made by myself and Sherman Burks.

Other Side Records also had a white girl duo called Party Girls. They were Surita and Shar. I remixed their song called *Stay Up* for the album. Surita and Shar were sisters and they liked to party so that's how they got their name. They were both Chicago girls.

It was good to have more females included in the growing House music scene. The girls had always been around but their stuff just wasn't as prominent as the men's stuff. There'd been Kym Mazelle and there'd been Xavier Gold who had sung on Ralphi Rosario's *You Used to Hold Me*. And there was also Adeva who was successful with her music. Juliet Roberts was also coming through strong too. Fans of House music have always liked divas and some people prefer the diva-style vocals to the males' vocals.

There have never been so many female producers. There's been more DJs. The ones that have stood out for me have been Angel and Princess Julia. Princess Julia had been one of the original Blitz Kids and really into fashion and music and hanging about with people like Boy George. Smokin Jo is another really good DJ. In fact she got the Number One DJ In The World award from *DJ Mag* back in the early 90s when she was really involved in the Ibiza scene that was exploding. I liked that the female DJs play a lot of melodic music that has a certain quality to it.

I don't know why there aren't so many female producers, it maybe that they lack a certain confidence in this area. I can only imagine they'd be just as good as any man. It would be good to see more women come through as producers but at this time they are still vastly outnumbered by the men in this field.

But men lack confidence too. Back in the days when I'd play the keyboards at forty bpm but then speed it up to 120 bpm everyone saw me do this and decided that they could do it too, but this was in America. The guys in the UK saw what I was doing but they lacked the confidence to try it and so they didn't make records like *Move Your Body*. Confidence is one of the big differences between America and the UK. America's got loads of confidence but the UK doesn't. I sometimes felt that the UK would look at what I was doing and think that what I was doing was too easy and that it really couldn't be that easy – but it was that easy. I only got started after I heard what Jesse Saunders was doing and I told myself that I could do better than that. Yeah, I think it came down to confidence. It's a certain kind of mentality.

Someone like Xavier Gold had that extra confidence because she was a singer and a DJ. But I don't think she had the confidence to make her own music. Xavier is a friend and I would love to work with her someday.

A friend of mine called Guy Wingate helped run Other Side Records with me. I couldn't be around all of the time because I was still working and travelling to gigs. Guy had been the editor of *Mixmag* and had some involvement with

KISS FM when it was still a pirate radio station. The second time around Other Side was mostly based in the UK. At that time Guy was very connected to what was happening in the world of dance music. He knew all the right people and where the Other Side Records releases needed to be marketed.

I had got to know Guy over the years that I had been coming to the UK. He'd been a journalist for *Mixmag* before he became the editor so we'd talked a lot about my music and House music and somewhere along the line about my record label, which he asked to get involved with and to which I agreed. Guy managed to do a great job with the label and he took it as far as he could.

It was just before Guy and I got together to re-launch Other Side Records that I took some time out from the music industry. It turned out to be a good two-year break. I had been working constantly since the mid 80s. I had had success with tracks like *Move You Body* and *Time Marches On*, plus there was all the Ten City, Kym Mazelle and Ce Ce Rogers stuff and I had been playing out all around the world and basically I had enough money to take a break from it all, so I decided that was what I was going to do. I needed to chill.

I just chilled, spent hours staring up at the ceiling and played video games. I was also in and out of relationships with a lot of women. But things were changing in this area too and this was partly related to AIDS. A friend of mine called Guy died which a lot of people said was related to AIDS. He was the first person that I had personally known to die from it. It really hit home and I was very sad because Guy and I were very close. There'd been a time when it had been me, Guy, Ce

Ce Rogers and Cedric Guy all hanging out together in New Jersey and it had been a really fun time. We'd go to all the clubs and party with the girls and the next thing we hear is that Guy is in the hospital and he's dying. After Guy died we all got really scared about our sexual relationships. Some of us got very monogamous after this time.

The AIDS thing had a huge impact in the States. People were dying because of it. By the end of the 80s people's awareness to AIDS had increased and people did start to take notice, be more careful and protect themselves. But throughout the 80s it was a really scary time for a lot of people involved in the club scenes. So although I was aware of it in the 80s, after Guy died I became very aware of it.

I heard about people dying from AIDS but didn't know many personally. I did know the Hip House artists Kool Rock Steady though. He had put out records like *Turn up the Bass* with Tyree and *Ain't We Funky Now* which had been released on DJ International. He died in 1996 from AIDS. Some people also said that Ron Hardy died because of AIDS but I don't know if that was true.

During my two-year break from the music business I didn't really miss too much about it. The thing I did miss was going into clubs and meeting new people. For years I had been used to meeting new faces every weekend and I hadn't realised just how big a part of my life that had become. Every weekend for the past five or six years I had gone to an airport, caught a flight to some country, I had been picked up by someone and they'd take me to a nice hotel. At the hotel I would chill for a little while before being taken to a nice restaurant for some dinner. I would have conversations, tell jokes, take the piss, talk about music, talk about Chicago or New York or London or any number of cities that I had been working in and then I would be taken to the club and I'd play my records. And every weekend I would fall in love. It was a very energetic period in my life.

It was also during this taking a break period that my dad died. It was cancer. Everyone in my family seems to die of cancer. My dad knew that he was dying. He paid off all of his bills. The man was a saint. By paying off all of his bills he set my mother up for life.

My dad was cremated in Chicago and a lot of people came to his funeral. I had no idea who a lot of those people even were. The ceremony lasted about four hours because people kept getting up and saying things about my dad. They talked about the favours that he'd done for them and how he had helped them. It was incredible. I just sat there and listened to them and – do you know what? – I just wasn't as sad as I thought I would be because of what those people were saying. I felt more proud than sad. My dad spent his life doing good deeds and on the day of the funeral all those people came to share their stories and say their goodbyes.

My dad was super proud of me too. He was always telling people about my career in the music industry and how I was travelling around the world and meeting lots of people and having records out that made people dance.

Another thing about my time-out period was that I didn't really take much notice about what was happening in the House world. I really did just chill and play video games and hang out with my various girlfriends. But of course House music continued to grow and develop and become a force to be reckoned with.

There were a few things that pulled me back into the music business. My dad dying was just contributing factor. Having spent two years just chilling I also needed to just get out again and move my body. So I started to move again and I haven't stopped moving since. I feel like I've been on a continual tour for the last twenty-five years. I feel like I'm living in a continuous state of jet lag. I just don't get any non jet lag days.

The first thing that I did after getting back in the game was to fly to the UK, play a few gigs and produce Tom Jones. I can't recall how this invite came about but I was totally into the idea because I loved Tom's voice.

At the time Tom was recording an album called *Tom Jones: The Lead And How To Swing It* and he wanted me to produce a song called *Love Is On Our Side*. We did the track in Olympic Studios in London. That was one of the major recording studios in the sixties, seventies and eighties. All the big groups recorded there: The Beatles, The Who, The Jam, U2. Sonique did a cover of the song too and that was included on her debut album. Up until then she'd been working with Mark Moore and S'Express.

I spent a few days working in that studio and while I was there Eric Clapton was also making music there and on another day Robert Plant and Jimmy Page came in, too. Tom told me that he knew Jimmy because back in the sixties he'd been a session guitarist for him. Tom asked me if I wanted to meet

Jimmy and Robert and I jumped at the chance. So I met Jimmy and Robert and they invited to me to their concert and they gave me back-stage passes. Fuck man, I had finally got to meet two of the members of Led Zeppelin, the band that had meant so much to me as a kid and which had been one of the reasons why I started to make music.

Tom Jones was so much fun. I enjoyed that time I spent with him. He was a very cool dude and I remember saying to him, 'Hey Tom, when you go back on tour and you get too many girls, you know you can send some my way', to which he replied, 'Marshall, there are never too many girls'.

It was around the time of getting back into music that I also found myself getting hooked up with the Church of Scientology and some of those guys were also back stage. One of those guys took a photograph of me with Led Zep. I don't have a copy of that photo and every time I ask for a copy they just tell me that I should go to one of their damn meetings.

I got interested in the Church of Scientology after reading the L. Ron Hubbard book *Dianetics: The Modern Science of Mental Health*. I would read it on the long flights that I was taking between gigs. I liked what I read and I thought wow, this is good shit. I felt that I wanted to get involved.

I started going to meetings at a Scientology centre on the Tottenham Court Road in London. When a new person joins up they have to go through an introductory process called the Purif otherwise known as the Purification Rundown. Essentially this is a detoxification programme that is meant to achieve certain outcomes that are beneficial to the individual.

So I was told I needed to do the Purif and I was like, What the fuck is that? They went to explain to me what it involves and the next thing I know I find myself doing a lot of exercise like running. I was also given niacin which is a nutriment because there's a whole dietary element to the Purif too. But I was only allowed to take the niacin with just water. This made my skin tingle. It's a very strange feeling. There's also intense sweating and they told me that this is required because it pushes out all the toxins in the body. It actually felt like that too. There was also a daily dose of hopping in the sauna too and you'd have to stay in there for long periods of time.

Now, I don't know if that shit worked or not but man I did feel good after doing it. I was also given an IQ test and which I hit about 125 on and then, after the purification rundown I was did it again, and it was 190. Admittedly, I did feel like I had more mental energy.

I got to meet a lot of interesting people through Scientology. There were these two girls in particular. They told me that they liked to do the Purif once a year but they weren't actually scientologists. I asked them why they weren't scientologists and why they did the Purif every year and they told me that they liked to get high. They said after a certain amount of time you didn't get high anymore and you would just smoke to feel normal. Well, after doing the Purif they got HIGH. They'd also realised that the first hit on a joint after doing the Purif was especially strong and blew the top of their heads off. The Church of Scientology also had a celebrity centre in London and I would go down there. There'd be some sexy chicks in that place.

Going into the 90s was a time when all the illegal raves had stopped in the UK. The government and the police had really come down heavy on the promoters and the pirate radio stations and they were confiscating their equipment, dishing out hefty fines and in some cases throwing people into prison, but despite this people still wanted to rave. By shutting down all the illegal parties what they achieved was to push all the ravers into clubs and that was when the super clubs got born. Clubs like Ministry of Sound, Cream, Hard Times and Back to Basics became the places to party.

Ministry of Sound is probably the best known of the clubs from that period and they have survived whereas many of the others haven't. The club was the idea of a guy called Justin Berkman. He'd wanted to create something like New York's Paradise Garage in London. In fact Larry Levan played at the club in its early days. Justin found a disused bus garage not far from the Elephant and Castle in London and turned it into Ministry of Sound. My dear friend Jazzy M was one of the first DJs to play at the club. Whenever I got booked to play at the club I would get the chance to hang out with Jazzy and that was always really good to do.

I found the super clubs like Ministry to be much more commercial than what had been before. They had a different vibe to, say, what had been in the clubs during the acid house period and in clubs like the Hacienda or Shoom. The shift in what was just a few years was quite staggering.

In the days of the illegal raves people didn't seem to give a fuck what they looked like or how they danced, but once the super clubs opened up there seemed to be all these supermodel-looking types everywhere. The people were just too good looking and I felt that something was missing. Something had changed. This was only in the UK though. You see the UK had had its underground House music scene but that was never the case in the States. We had the Chicago throng with clubs like the Warehouse and the Music Box but the majority of clubs were already commercial and the people that went to those clubs always looked good. We didn't have raves in the States, not in the late 80s anyway. Anything that resembled a rave only came about going into the 2000s when EDM came about.

What the super clubs also did was to make House music mainstream. Ministry of Sound really capitalised on this and they started putting out compilation album after compilation album. They turned what had been just a club in London into a global brand which is still going strong today.

Entering the 90s was also when people started to give names to music like hard core, jungle, trance, drum and bass. I saw this happening and was left asking the question, How is anybody going get any sales from their music once everything gets split into sub-genres? When House music first started you had everything on one dance floor. It was cool shit when you had everything in one place. You could have a rap song and if it was cool it was House, if you had any cool song, it was House. But new sub-genres got formed and things started to get split up. I actually felt that making these genres was unimaginative. I thought the people behind it were formatting themselves and at the same time strangling themselves.

I did a lot of the records that came out of that period. However, I did think that for every one good song there were a hundred bad songs that had been made just for the sake of being able to call it a jungle record or a drum and bass record. Once it got like that there was a lot of corny shit put out there.

If I liked something from any of these new genres I would play it. I thought it was House I would play it. Getting back out there playing again I would have records like *Everyday Thang* by Melanie Williams, the sweet mercy mix and *Giving It Up* by Incognito, the Roger Sanchez mix. There was still a lot of good music out there that got people dancing.

People started calling and labelling my music as Deep House. I didn't come up with that. I never quite understood it and to me House just meant House. Deep House was just another sub-genre that someone came up with to describe my feel of music but I've never tried to understand what it means. I guess what they're trying to describe is cool house, heavy house and something with meaning and makes people think. I guess my personality comes through my music. I've always felt that an artist should inject themselves into their music. My attitude is that you should be able to tell the difference from me and say Farley and you should be able to tell Farley from Adonis and so on. When House music started we did that and people could tell the difference. Nowadays someone puts a record out and you can't tell who the fuck it is.

The problem with a lot of today's music is that there is no personality in it. There's no room left for personality in music. The music industry is really lacking personality. People have been forced to lose their identity and it leaves me feeling sad.

I would like people to appreciate the artists and the producers and be able to say, 'Wow, that's a jam from so and so'. Now people just say 'Wow that's a jam' and they have no idea who the artist or producer is.

Some of the problem comes down to the equipment that the studios use and some of it is the record labels needs. A record label attempts to make a niche for themselves. They think they need an identity and this means after they've had one successful song every other song, from whatever artist, has to sound like that one song. This limits progress and it suffocates the artists and the producers. So many songs today sound the same and it stifles creativity. Record labels are forever just getting this guy or that guy into remix the same record and then they sell that.

Record labels pull in big guys who they know will get the clicks and clicks mean sales. There's something like a hundred thousand songs being released a week and if that record doesn't sound like anything else and be compared to such or such song and it doesn't have a big name producer on it, it just ain't going to get any clicks, or at least enough clicks to get the public's attention.

It's a huge problem and I would like to say it's going to change for the better but things have become so locked in, it's hard to see if anything can change. It would take a significant event to change anything now and I don't know what that could be. I just tell record label guys that they should promote their artists and their images or they'll just get lost in a very large pool.

How do I get to hear and discover new music? Mostly these days that will happen when I go out to play. I'll be in the club and the DJ who is on either before or after me will play something that I like and I think that's good, who is that? What I'll then do is Shazam it and find out what it is and I'll go a buy it.

To be honest discovering new music doesn't excite me like it used to. The reason is that it's too easy to get now. It only takes a couple of mouse clicks and you've got that new song. Back in the 80s when I was starting out as a DJ getting hold of a new record was a really exciting thing. You had to make effort to get records then. I mean you had to actually get off the sofa and go to a record store. There was one compilation album called *Mixed Energy* with a song called *Haven't Been Funked Enough* by Ex Tras. Now nobody had this record. What I did was I tracked down the record label that had put the record out and I told them who I was and that I loved the record and was playing out in Chicago and they sent me twenty-five copies. After I had played the record out I gave copies to members of the Hot Mix 5 just because I could beat the Hot Mix 5 playing the record first. I remember those guys came over to my house to pick their records out.

I do feel sad for the kids that just aren't going to experience that kind of excitement that I did as a kid. The worrying thing is that it's unlikely that they ever will. They are not being encouraged to make an effort to go and get new music. I don't as much anymore. One of the last songs I made an effort to go and get was called *Stay* by the Layabouts and Imaani. I heard another DJ play that, I shazammed it and I went out and tracked it down. It's a really good song. Another example is a song called *Way Back* by Amber Mark. This is a really good song with some nice piano and vocals. It's not your average House beat song but I like to play it out and do a radio mix and throw on some special effects and it makes it feel much faster and people dance.

CHAPTER TEN

I can vividly recall the inventive vibes just like yesterday. The ideas that consumed our jam session together, all began on an Akai MPC. Marshall and I brainstormed collectively for the song 69%, prior to finalizing and recording it in the studio. Marshall has not only set the tone and soundstage for quality House music of his era; but he has also created a unique and profound art form for many generations to come. Marshall has paved the way for various artists, through his eccentric style and intriguing designs. His remarkable talents are implemented throughout his work in countless ways. He continues to illustrate, collaborate and conduct masterpieces. His hard work, creativity and dedication has been the additional drive and fuel to his amazing craft. I give my utmost respect, appreciation and thanks for his inspiration. I define Marshall as a peaceful personality, without star allures. Overall, a true Dalai Lama of House music.
Serge Imhof

I was also putting out records again and in 1992 I did *Message 2 Ron* under Club MCM and Marshall Jefferson. This was released on Rhythm Beat Records. This song was done by K-

Alexi Shelby and we spoke recently about it. The song related to Ron Hardy who had recently died and was meant to be some kind of tribute to him.

K-Alexi and me used to share a house together in Chicago. In fact there was a few of us who lived in it. There was me, K-Alexi, Bam Bam, Reggie Hall, Mike Dunn, Sherman Burks, Chauncey Alexander and Gershon Jackson. Somehow we all managed to live together under this one roof in the South Side of the city.

Most of the time it was a fucking madhouse. We'd also have people coming over all the time just to hang out, people like Farley, Lil Louis, Armando and Maurice Joshua often came to hang out. At some point just about everybody in the Chicago House music industry came paid us a visit. Some people would also come over to work with us too because we had our equipment in the basement, which K-Alexi named the Dungeon.

Because everybody combined their equipment we had a pretty good set-up and we were able to make records. I wrote the entire first Ten City in that house. Bam Bam wrote *Where's Your Child* there. He also wrote *Give It To Me* and that came about after he heard me say to my girlfriend Esther 'give it to me baby'. For some reason he thought that was funny and I still tease him about it to this day.

Living in that house with all those guys was sensational. Someone was always grabbing you so that they could play you their latest song that they'd just written or started to write. It was also a very competitive place to be, but it was a healthy competition, which we all got off on.

When girls were brought back to the house we'd tell them that we were going to take them down into the dungeon. K-Alexi even had a separate room in the dungeon and he'd bring girls back and we would be able to hear the noises coming from the room.

In 1994 I did a song called *Sunshine n' Your Eyes*. This was put out under Interstate Records, who was Woody and the guys. They called me up asking if I'd make a record for them. It had a crazy keyboard part and a vocalist singing 'I see the sun' on the intro.

Soon after *Sunshine n' Your Eyes* was *I Found You* which I wrote with JD Braithwaite. This song was put out on Centrestage Records, which was a UK label run by Andrew 'Doc' Livingstone and Simon Marks. Andrew asked me if I wanted to put a record out with him and I agreed.

JD has put out some really good songs like *Ready For Love* and *Sound of Music*. I really loved JD's vocals. I worked with JD as co-producers on another song that Centrestage put out and that was called *These Emotions* by Merleen Allen.

My other release from around that time was *Far Behind* by Idle and Wild. This was me and Keith Thompson. Keith was the guy that sang on *Break 4 Love* by Raze which was a massive hit back in 1989. It was Keith, Curtis McClain and myself who sang the vocals on *Far Behind*. We recorded the song at Broadley Studios in London and the record was put out by Hott Records, which was a garage house label owned by Alan Russell.

It was Keith who came up with the name Idle and Wild. I don't know if I was meant to be idle or wild. Keith is a really nice guy and we had a ball while making that record.

Keith also sang backing vocals on the record *Step By Step* which came out on Freetown Records in 1995. This was a song put out under Marshall Jefferson featuring Curtis McClain. The remix was done by Ron Trent.

It was great to work with Curtis again. He flew into London to do the song. It had been a decade since he'd sang on *Move Your Body*. Throughout all this time we'd stayed friends and we'd kept an eye on what we were both doing with our lives. Curtis hadn't been able to make a career in the music industry. He'd had to keep on doing jobs back in Chicago. He stayed involved with House music but it wasn't enough to live on.

I hooked up with JD Braithwaite again to do some songs with Zeki Lin. A total of four tracks were recorded but it never got released. I think JD sang on two of the songs but I recall we removed his vocals on one of the songs.

Zeki Lin was my flatmate during a time when I was living in London. Now Zeki was a Turkish guy. He had a flat in Chelsea which was in Walpole Street, just off of the Kings Road.

I ended up staying with Zeki after arriving in London and having nowhere to stay. A friend of mine, Carl Bias from Master C&J hooked me up with Zeki and he said I could stay at his flat for a few days. I gave Zeki something £250 and after a few days told him that I was going to find a hotel. Zeki told me that there was no need to go and get a hotel and we came

193

to an agreement where I could stay at the flat. Our arrangement suited both of us and we both got along really well. I ended staying in that flat in Chelsea with Zeki for three years.

While I lived with Zeki he had a job being a DJ at a club called Annabel's. Annabel's was an exclusive club in an old Georgian mansion in Berkeley Square. As a private members' club those guys were paying something like ten thousand pounds annually. A lot of celebrities use the place because they know they can pretty much be left alone.

Zeki got the job after being spotted by the owner of Annabel's playing a DJ set back in Turkey. They liked what they heard and invited Zeki to be a resident DJ at the club and, on top of that, they had given him the flat in Walpole Street to use too as part of the deal. So Zeki was living rent free and getting a salary as well. He had got real lucky.

Zeki had also been in the Turkish army and one of his roles was to drive a really high-up general around. One time George Bush Senior went to Turkey and the general threw a party and Zeki was asked to be the DJ. In fact I think the general ordered Zeki to arrange the party, so he ended organising it too. By all accounts the party was that amazing that George Bush asked to meet Zeki and so Zeki got to meet George Bush. Bush even arranged a visa to America for Zeki, so he was got a lifetime visa to the USA out of throwing that party too.

While living in that Chelsea flat there were a lot of Turkish people that came to visit Zeki. When some of them visited they'd hang around and get high. There was one occasion when a few of these guys laughed and joked at me for not joining in with them as they got high and they blew smoke at me. Now, I was flying out to Chicago that same day and as I was going through security the dogs sniffed me out and I got asked to step to onside.

This was one of the few times I have ever used the 'I'm Marshall Jefferson the Godfather of House Music' because they were getting serious and searching through everything and breaking out the rubber gloves. That certainly got my attention and I started yelling, 'But I'm Marshall Jefferson the Godfather of House Music!' It was close but they didn't use the rubber gloves in the end and they let me out of there.

The funny thing now is that those guys who blew smoke in my face are now high up in the Turkish Government.

As good as the deal was that Zeki was getting at Annabel's he hit a time when he wanted to get out. I think he felt kinda locked into what he was doing there and needed a change. I think he saw making a record with me as a means to get out. I don't think he realised though what sort of money he'd need to be making from making music and releasing records that would compare to his working for Annabel's situation.

I think Zeki's frustration came from not being able to play House music the way he wanted to. This was because he was playing at a private members' club and those guys were always going up to him and making requests that he'd have to honour. I mean if you'd have Brad Pitt coming into the club and asking you to play the Rolling Stones then you play the Rolling Stones.

I had the freedom to play whatever the fuck I wanted to and he saw that and because he knew he couldn't it got him down. But he had the flat in Chelsea and salary so it wasn't too bad.

Thankfully I have only had minor incidents at airports, nothing too serious with security. I don't take any chances because I need to fly for my living. I've had stuff that has been lost though. There's been occasions when my whole box of records has gone missing. One of the main reasons why I stopped playing vinyl was because I was getting fed up with my records getting scratched and damaged as they went through the baggage-handling process.

Vinyl has become a precious commodity. The days when a label would press up ten or twenty thousand copies is long gone. At the time when I stopped playing vinyl some labels were only pressing up five hundred copies or sometimes even less. This meant that if your record got damaged it might be hard to find a replacement.

Nowadays when I buy vinyl it goes straight to digital and put the record away for safe keeping. I spend time re-mastering the song to make it sound the way I want it to sound and it's ready for me to play out.

I managed to last until 2008 before I stopped playing vinyl. Up until then I dug my heels in and refused to play anything else. But something had to change so I made that change to suit my work.

After 2008 I was playing CDs. The problem was the songs didn't always sound too great in the clubs. This was often because the soundman didn't know what the fuck he was doing. Often it just seemed like the soundman was the promoter's friend and he'd been brought in for that reason only. I can't tell you how many guys I have come across who don't know how to organise a stereo sound system.

These days when I travel to gigs I have USB sticks in my pocket. Each USB stick has 8000 songs on it. I have enough songs for any occasion. I usually carry four USB sticks. One serves as a back-up and then I have a back-up for that and then another back-up for the back-up. Back in 1986 I never thought I'd be travelling the world with all my songs on tiny pieces of plastic that fitted into my pocket.

What I liked about the mid 90s was that there was still lots of new music coming out and DJs were in demand. Faithless put a song out called *God is a DJ* and for a while people were really going nuts for DJs.

I actually really enjoyed that period and one of the things that made that time so great to be a DJ was the festivals. At those festivals you would always be bumping into other DJs and we all got to know one another and have a great time. There was a lot of fun and a lot of money flying around too.

The DJs around at the time were all really funny guys too. I can't recall any very serious guys. So a lot of fun was being had and a lot of good events and festivals were happening. The guys I remember hanging out with were: Brandon Block, Carl Cox, Paul Okenfold, Paul Van Dyke, Doctor, Roger Sanchez, Louis Vega, Derrick May, West Bam and Dr Motte – he was the guy that started the Love Parade.

The 90s was the first time when some real money was getting paid out to DJs. Some guys were commanding anywhere between ten and twenty-five thousand pounds for a night. Festival gigs paid more than clubs too.

The most I have ever known a DJ to be paid was one million dollars. This was the fee given to Deadmau5 for a residency in Las Vegas. Junior Vasquez also got paid one million pounds for playing one night at Wembley Stadium. Now that is a huge amount of money.

I have played at numerous festivals. Glastonbury is among them. I didn't really like it though. Back when I went in the 90s it didn't appear to be that well organised and at the time was the shittiest festival that I played at. It looks better now but then the DJ thing is of lesser importance too, it's gone back to bands.

I especially liked the Tribal Gathering festivals. There was one called Big Love that I have fond memories of. The guys behind Tribal Gatherings really did manage to create something special. Their events would pull into twenty-five thousand ravers and they got the best DJs and acts in, with the likes of Leftfield and the Chemical Brothers and I believe they even had Kraftwerk headline at one of their events too. In 1996 I was asked to present a mix of a bunch of songs for a Tribal Gathering compilation album. This was my first mix album. In the mix I included tracks like: *Happy Days* by Alexander Hope, *Be Free* by Basement Jazz and my *Jump On It*. Gayle San and James Lavelle provided the mixes for the other two CDs included on that box set.

Another event I really enjoyed was in Zurich, Switzerland. This was called the Street Parade. There were half a million people at that event, so it was a huge affair. That was special for me because I felt that I really ripped it up that night.

I played a song and Armand Van Helden saw me play it and later he sampled it and made a song of his own out of it. I remember all the other DJs came to watch me play my set and because I tore it up, I felt really good.

In the 90s I was aware that artists like Faithless, the Chemical Brothers and Moby were making an impact on the dance music scene. They'd all come out of the late 80s rave culture and had started to create their own thing. But to be honest I didn't really know too much about them or what they were doing. I was busy doing my own thing.

I have met Moby a couple of times. I saw him in Germany at the Love Parade and he wasn't playing that chilled-out stuff, he was playing hard core techno and I mean hard core techno. He was the man! The crowd was dancing so fast I was wondering if they'd turn to light. It was wild!

I enjoyed living in London and there were many highpoints. I also found getting around to be really easy. From where I was staying in Chelsea access to the rest of the city was easy. It was only a short walk to Sloane Square Tube station. The tubes came along every couple of minutes. London has the best transportation system that I have ever come across. I sussed this quickly and from then on used the Tube to get around all of the time rather than waving down taxis. London was nothing like Chicago. I mean back in Chicago you have to wait for the L-train for something like thirty minutes.

When I wasn't working I went shopping. Shopping is what I liked to do during the daytime. I would go and search for electrical items, video games and records. There were a few record shops where I would go but most of the time it would be Jazzy M's Vinyl Zone and Black Market Records in Soho.

Soho was a unique place. I couldn't really compare it to anything like we had back in Chicago. I liked going there and hanging out with the guys who worked in Black Market like Nicky and Frankie. It was a pretty cool place to go and unlike the record stores in Chicago you were allowed to listen to the records before you bought them. This wasn't the custom in Chicago. Back home you basically had to take their word that it was a good record as they'd say, 'Buy this coz it's a hot cut'. You had to take those guys' word and trust them that it was a 'hot cut'. But in Black Market they had some decks and you could select a record and you could play it to see if you liked it or not, and I thought that was wild.

If I wasn't working but just wanted to hang out. I liked to go to the Ministry of Sound or Queer Nation, which was a club night where you'd see Norman Jay or Princess Julia or the Rhythm Doctor.

Another thing about London was that I thought all the girls looked like supermodels – especially around the Chelsea and Sloane Square areas. I mean just walking down the Kings Road would blow your mind because of all the gorgeous girls. I got the impression that some of those girls were trying to catch the wealthy guys, who also lived in the area.

But in between watching the pretty girls, hanging out in clubs and record shops, playing video games and going shopping and jumping on the Tube I continued to make music and *Jump On It* was a record that I released in 1996. This was put out by KTM Records and Other Side Records. It was also included on my album called *Day of the Onion* that was released the same year.

I recorded the whole album in Frankfurt for KTM which stood for Keep Things Movin'. I had originally been dealing with Tresor which was a record label that took its name from a techno club in Berlin, but they moved my album onto their sub-label which was KTM and they were linked to Interfisch. KTM put out records by other guys like my friend from back in Chicago Vince Lawrence and my Chelsea flatmate, Zeki Lin.

Dimitri Hegemann ran the label and it was arranged that I used some recording studios in Frankfurt, so I flew out there. The DJ and producer and record label owner Chris Leibing, who was from Frankfurt, allowed me to use an apartment that he had there.

It took me just one week to record *Day of the Onion*. Each day I would go into the studio and work. There'd be just me. I played everything on the album. It was pretty straightforward and I wrote everything from scratch on a day to day basis. Before going into the studio I had nothing waiting to be recorded, so each day was spent composing, playing and mixing the songs. Ten tracks found their way onto the album. Among them were *Party Time*, *Floating*, *Funk in Outer Space*, *Jump on It* and *Day of the Onion*.

The songs on the album came out of some simple jams really. There wasn't much of a concept to it at all. All of the songs were instrumentals so I didn't need to come up with any lyrics.

Back in Chicago when you see a girl with a great ass, you'd say, 'Look at the onion on that girl'. So, *Day of the Onion* is a reference to that and the day a girl gets to shake their booty.

Day of the Onion was my first album and this was ten years after *Move Your Body: The House Music Anthem* had been released. I hadn't been asked in the past and no one was really offering much money to do an album anyway. KTM were going to pay me so I agreed to make an album. The other thing was that I had never really perceived myself as being an artist. I considered myself to be a producer and a DJ.

I had a good time making the album and staying in Frankfurt and hanging out with the German guys. I had got to know Chris Liebing because we did the song *Mushrooms* together. Chris was part of Noosa Heads with Andrew Wooden and *Mushrooms* was put out by Soap Records, which was the same label that had put out their track called *Basis*.

It was during one of those sessions in Frankfurt, hanging out with Chris, that he asked me to go down to the studio with him. I went into the booth and tested the microphone and while I did this I told Chris the story of meeting those girls in my college days and going to Florida and taking the mushrooms with them. He liked the story and he recorded it. The song came out with me telling the story about the girl inviting me to eat a mushroom and the next thing 'I'm walking on clouds' and 'feeling like I had no feet' as I walked on those 'beautiful clouds'. It's basically me describing how wonderful I felt.

I really like Germany. I have played there countless times and stayed in numerous places. I'm especially fond of their food. I remember a particular train station where they had the most incredible sauerkraut dish for sale. Now sauerkraut is a made of finely cut cabbage. The derogatory term for Germans 'kraut' comes from the dish's name. I think the British and Americans came up with that during World War One. The dish I got came with potatoes and some magnificent sausages, and they have been the greatest sausages that I have ever tasted. I had them sausages every day that I was staying in that area.

After recording *Day of the Onion* I actually ended up staying in Germany for a few months. I moved away from Frankfurt to stay in another city called Duisberg. This happened because I had met a girl. I then moved and stayed at a hotel in Berlin owned by Tresor Records. People called the place Hotel Sandman. This was because rooms in that place were small and all you could really do in them was to go to sleep. Each room only had a bed in it. There wasn't room any other pieces of furniture, not even a TV. In fact you could hardly fit the bed in to it.

Hotel Sandman was very basic and the rooms didn't even have toilets or showers in them, they were located down the hall and shared with everyone else. It was clean and well maintained though and so I stayed there for a good couple of months.

While staying at Hotel Sandman I got myself a bicycle and I used that to get around Berlin. I spent a lot of time in the Kreuzberg area. This was where the artistic types hung out.

People like David Bowie and Iggy Pop used to hang out there and there was a punk club called SO36 which was the Berlin equivalent of New York's CBGBs. That area also helped to make hip hop popular in Germany, too.

Within a few weeks of staying at the Hotel Sandman I had decided to install a TV in my room and, because I read books on a daily basis, I put up a shelf for the books. I was reading a lot of *Star Trek* novels back then. I even put in a small sound system. When I moved on I left all that stuff in that room and when I returned a few months later I learned that everyone was calling that room the Marshall Jefferson Suite. They had the Marshall Jefferson library, the Marshall Jefferson transportation and the Marshall Jefferson TV and music system.

I liked Berlin and I liked having a bike to 'get into the creases' of the city. When you move around an unfamiliar city in a taxi or on their subway system you miss a lot of what the place has to offer. On a bike you get a different feel and you stumble across things that you just wouldn't expect. Something else I liked about Kreuzberg was that everyone from the artistic community seemed to know one another. This was a very different experience to living in London. In Chelsea, people seemed pretty private and didn't talk to each other. What I do remember about Kreuzberg is the dog shit. They let their dogs shit everywhere.

Another guy I hung about with a lot was Dr Motte. When he'd started the Love Parade there was only about 150 people that turned out for it. It was simple and basic, just a few people dancing in the street to a sound system.

Dr Motte told me that he started the Love Parade after hearing my song *Open Your Eyes*. He said it made him and his people feel loved and they wanted to share that, so they took the music out onto the street. At first when he told me that I thought he'd lost his marbles a bit but I appreciated the gesture. But as he described it to me it reminded me of the UK's Second Summer of Love from 88/89.

The following year the Love Parade festival attracted a few thousand people and then it reached something like 50,000 and then as they continued to spread the love and share the music it got up to 2,000,000 people dancing in the streets of Berlin. The festival had its problems though and in the summer of 2010 twenty-one people were crushed in a tragic stampede incident. This was the last Love Parade. It's a shame the Love Parade had to come to an end under such horrible circumstances and I always enjoyed playing there.

CHAPTER ELEVEN

Marshall and I have known each other for over thirty years, but we really don't know each other, but we really are each other. In thirty years we've had one meal together, one long car drive together, gone shopping together once, watched a movie together once, mixed each other's music without the other's knowledge, and we still haven't deejayed together. It's been an amazing time with my Brother-in-House.

I first met Marshall right after Move Your Body *came out. There hadn't been as much excitement about a new record in Chicago since I released* Time *to* Jack *and* It's House. *Marshall brought in the evolution of the blueprint I created. Just by adding piano, in a way he legitimized it. Now it wasn't just dance music, it was music. I think we met at the DJ International office, and there were some reporters and they wanted to know about House fashion and lifestyle. Marshall and I didn't know each other but when I say we ARE each other, we instantly knew we had to take this English guy to the South Side of Chicago to the infamous Evergreen Plaza Shopping Mall. From the Lark to Bigsby and Kruthers, we showed him what the kids were wearing to school and at the clubs. Marshall and I were on the same page with everything, just as if we'd been scripted or known each other since childhood. Marshall always remembers the drive because I was in one of my sports cars, and driving a tiny bit fast and furious. I think it was that same day that I was asked to do a mix on the second release of* Move Your Body. *My mix was uncredited, and unpaid as well. It's the one with the samples. The one that starts off "gotta have, gotta have" etc, and then goes into drums. Funny, most DJs I know said that's their favourite mix, It's not Marshall's. LOL*

I think the next time I'd hang with Marshall would be ten years or so later. We were both in San Francisco and out of the blue, he told me that I needed to see Lord of the Rings. *Um...OK. So we did. Then I found out it was his second or third time seeing it. If Marshall isn't sleeping or playing music, he's probably watching a movie. If you want to get next to him, don't offer him women or drugs or even money, offer him a great movie and you're in. Fast forward another ten years or so and Marshall and I are both in Berlin. We decide to meet and have dinner before our gigs (at different venues). We enjoy the meal, have great conversation, and go to do our thing. That was 2016. Now over the years (especially since social media) we've kept in touch via email, messages and few phone calls. From the beginning to this day, it's just been easy for us to relate to each other. Why? Because we are Chicago, we are House. We have a special bond that most people will never understand. I'm looking forward to this December, we've finally been booked to play together at the same venue, equal headliners, Brothers-in-House. I love what you've brought to OUR sound. Peace.* Chip E

So many years after first hearing *On And On* by Jesse Saunders an opportunity arose for us to work together and, despite not really liking working with people, I was certainly going to make an exception for Jesse. The track we made was called *Of Love*. I did a mix and Jesse did a mix called *Jesse's Deep Throat Mix*. We did that song in Neckargemund, which is in Heidenberg, Germany. It's a very beautiful place. The Neckar River flows through the area and it's one of my favourite holiday spots. I remember the swans floating on the water. There were three restaurants there too and at night they would be lit up by candles. It was a most amazing sight. The roads were old and made of cobblestones. It was a very romantic place to go and I'd sometimes take the ladies there.

I was buzzing the whole time I was working with Jesse. I mean I was only in the gang of making House music because of Jesse. In the studio we clicked. Jesse gave me my space and I gave Jesse his.

In the years since *On And On* and *Move Your Body* we'd both been very busy. We'd continued to make music and tour and for some reason Jesse had also ended up spending some time in Germany. It was this that provided the opportunity for us to make music together.

Jesse had been interviewed for a book called *What Kind of House Party Is This* and it had explained that he was responsible for House music and off the back of that I believe he was getting offered work in Europe and so found his way into Germany too. Jesse also wrote his own book called *House Music: The Real Story* and this has been very well received.

Both Jesse and I also got involved with the Chicago House Music Tour that went around Germany. The other guys on the tour were Roy Davies, Felix the House Cat, Mike Dunn, DJ Pierre and possibly Armando too. An organisation called Love To Love arranged the tour. This was a couple called Conti and Rosetta. They were very sweet people. I had so much fun hanging out with the guys on that tour. We had a ball.

Each night was jam packed with all of us DJs playing our sets. We also did a lot of travelling and a lot of staying in hotels. To help with the chill-out periods we bought TVs. Mike Dunn was the first to go out and buy one and, once we saw that he had one, we all went out and bought one. But they got mad at me because I told them that they wouldn't be able to use their TVs because the electrical formats were different to what they were understood. You have either NTSC or PAL. It's to do with the way something gets broadcast. The outcome was that everybody had to leave their TVs in Germany.

It was on that tour that I first met Ronald 'Ron' Trent. He'd been getting a lot of attention since his first release *The Afterlife* with tracks like *Foot Therapy* and *A Dark Room And A Feeling*. Ron was also a Chicago guy but being much younger than me I hadn't known him from back in the day. Another guy I got to know was Robert Armani. Like Ron he was also from Chicago and he was a similar age to Ron. We got along and hung out. Robert released songs like *Fuse Box* and *Hard Work* in the mid 90s.

The first time I met Robert he was standing at the hotel reception desk completely naked. He was as calm as if he was just waiting in the checkout queue in the grocery store. He turned to me and said, 'Hi, Marshall right?' and he introduced himself. I was just thinking, I'm not going to forget this guy. It turned out that he had sleepwalked right out of his hotel room and locked the door behind him.

In 1996 I also had a track released called *Touch the Sky*. There was four mixes put out and one was mixed by Zeki Lin. There was a guy called Sangki involved with me around this time too and he was very interesting. He ran a label called Free Town Inc when he came to London with sixteen million pounds in his pocket. The story went that he was a bookkeeper for the Korean mafia but decided he'd needed to get out of it, so he chose England as the place to make his new home.

Everybody loved Sangki because wherever he went around London he got everyone high. Cocaine was a big thing in London in the mid 90s. I can only imagine that Sangki spent a lot of his sixteen million during that period.

Artists also liked to work with Sangki and his record label because when he asked you to make a record he'd also ask you how much did you want and he'd never argue with anyone's price. Producers would say they wanted five grand and he'd be shoving this into their hands without batting an eyelid. Sangki put out records for Masters At Work, Ron Trent and Little Louie Vega. I'm not even sure he liked the music but he did like hanging out with the various artists on his label.

Sangki and I also started to hang out quite a bit. We'd go to movies and stuff and he liked being with me because I was one of the few guys in his life that didn't want to get high because I was still abstaining from drug use. I guess he figured out that by hanging out with me he could have some respite from the hectic druggy lifestyle that he was surrounded by. Being with me meant that he could just relax and just enjoy being straight for a few hours.

Everybody did love Sangki though and people were genuinely upset when they heard that he had died in a car crash. Now he owned a really dodgy car. There was something not right with the steering wheel and it was always giving him problems.

On the day he had that car crash he also had some other guys that I knew. There was John Robertson who I knew from New York and another guy too and they also died. The thing was I also supposed to have been in that car because I was meant to be on that trip with them. That day Sangki had called me up asking me to go and hang out with him and the others and he had a plan that would include taking a trip in his car. I had declined saying that I just really needed to chill and I recall he was practically begging me to go, but I remained firm in my decision and I'm glad that I did.

Going into 1997 KTM released the Animals EP. Dimitri Hegemann was full of ideas. He had a history of trying to do things with his wacky ideas. When I first met him he had a company called Space Beer. He had a really good set up with it and lots of marketing ideas 'Space Beer – have a nice flight'. I actually introduced Dimitri to some advertising executive guys that Vince Lawrence hooked me up with. Those guys went berserk over Space Beer and told Dimitri that they may be able to secure him a multimillion deal. They flew Dimitri into Chicago and put him in meetings with some really big guys from the advertising world and they were very keen for his German beer. But Dimitri called me to tell me what was happening and how those guys just kept talking about the money and he said, 'Marshall they just talk about money but what about the heart, what about the soul?' I simply replied, 'Dimitri you can buy a lot of hearts and a lot of souls with the millions they're going to give you, man.'

He turned down all of their offers.

Another brilliant idea that Dimitri had was what inspired the Animals EP. At the time I was staying at Hotel Sandman and he'd invited me over to his home for the evening. During the course of the evening he told me that he was going to build a gigantic Trojan horse. His intention was to take this horse around different cities in Germany and then onto the rest of Europe and then the rest of the world. His idea was that there'd be a sound system built inside the horse and it would blast out techno music.

With the idea of Dimitri's Trojan horse in mind I made the song called *The Horse (Is Coming)*. I liked Dimitri's vision and I wanted to honour it. Dimitri did actually build the horse but he ended up facing problems and barriers from the various city authorities that prevented him being able to take it on the road. I guess those cities couldn't understand Dimitri's vision and were too scared to have a load of kids dancing in their streets to a big Trojan horse that played techno music.

The other song on the Animal's EP was *The Cow (Is Already Waiting)*. Like *The Horse*, *The Cow* was also an up-tempo instrumental. *The Horse* was a pretty good song but I think *The Cow* was the better of the two.

Not too long after The Animal's EP I did *I Got Da Feeling*. The guys at Strawberry Records wanted a song and they approached me and, offered me some money, so I did it. The A-side was the club mix and we called that the Strawberry Side and the B-side was called the Cream Side and that had two other mixes of the song; the heat mix and the dub mix. Strawberry Records was a British House music label that had been putting out records since the early part of the 90s.

I only had a couple of records released in 98 and one of those was a track called *One More Chance* which I teamed up with Jesse Saunders again to do. The German label UCA Records was behind this release and it was put out as Marshall Jefferson and Jesse Saunders. There was another version also released featuring Tyree Cooper, Farley 'Jackmaster' Funk and Screamin' Rachael, all people I had known from the Chicago and Trax Records days. Tyree did the rapping on the song and Screamin' Rachael did a vocal, but I had nothing to do with that version. It was such a buzz making that record with Jesse. Just being in the same studio was special.

The only other release of 98 was *Feed the Lions (Blakkat Mix)* which was done as Kaligula on Pleasure, who were based in Manchester. I wrote the song with a guy called Mark Bell. Mark was very much into his acid house and he also ran a record label of his own too. He's a very talented guy. Mark did all the music on *Feed the Lions* and I did the vocals. Mark was from Blackpool and so we ended up recording the track there. I have to say I didn't go too much on Blackpool. I thought it was one ugly-assed city. Mark had several kids and I remember his wife at the time talked like Popeye. Things didn't work out for Mark though and he left his wife and kids and he went to the black hole. I call California the black hole because so many of my friends have gone there and they've never come back.

The 90s for me was a time when there was a lot of money being tossed around. There seemed to be plenty of money for everyone in the House music scene. It was in this decade when the major record labels started to put out House music and DJs really were perceived as being gods by a lot of kids. The 90s was the era of the superstar DJ and lots of guys just blew up and became household names. By the end of the 90s House music had taken over the world and people were still dancing to the songs that we had made all those years earlier back in Chicago. Going into the 2000s there looked like there was going to be lots of opportunities and it was an exciting time to be making House music.

CHAPTER TWELVE

Most of my interaction with Marshall was in the late 80s and then into the 90s. This was really because House was such a revolution and he was one of the first around. There were other people like Steve 'Silk' Hurley who had Jack Your Body *but it was Marshall who was the real 'big' name from that Chicago House music scene. I got to know Marshall because he started to get brought over the UK by a guy called Patrick Lilly. He ran High On Hope back in the day. I got to know Marshall quite well and I found that not only his music making was an enigma but his personality was too. He was a very interesting person and a very 'cool' cat who I remember always wore a long black leather coat and he had a sort of crazy hair thing going on too. I found him to be humble and I think this was because at the time he wasn't properly recognised back on his own turf. Even though there was a House music history being built back in Chicago with clubs like the Warehouse and in New York with the Paradise Garage, the actual scene was very small. This meant that when Marshall came to the UK and got the response that he did, he was really chuffed, as well as being humble. And he was making some of the most influential House music records ever – but he certainly wasn't full of himself about it.* Judge Jules

I have lived and stayed in so many places throughout my career and I have enjoyed many of those places, but my roots always feel like they are back in Chicago.

I have also lived with so many different people and I mostly have a lot of fond memories connected to them. Memories of the time spent with my dear friend Ce Ce Rogers always bring smiles to my face.

I'd known Ce Ce since 1987 and, when we had done *Someday* together. You know he sang that vocal in one take and that was used on the record? The guy is unbelievable. Around the time of *Someday* I was touring a lot in the East Coast area. Ce Ce lived in East Orange, New Jersey and he said it was okay that I stayed with him. We became best buddies because of that period but the clincher was when I met Ce Ce's mother. She was loud and outspoken, just like my mother. Whenever I spent time with her she'd tell embarrassing stories about Ce Ce. I remember she told me one about how Kenneth (that's his real name) broke the chair in the church when he sat on it because he was so fat. The thing was when Ce Ce came to Chicago to hang with me and meet my mother, she would also tell embarrassing stories about me. We'd both laugh about that.

Ce Ce and me would go to the clubs in East Orange and we could see the guys pulling away their girlfriends. They felt threatened because we seemed to have some kind of reputation of stealing other guys' girls. The guys would give us that look which says 'please man, stay away from my woman'.

House music was huge in New Jersey, the people there really embraced what we had been doing in Chicago. After Ce Ce did *Someday* he became the House king of East Orange. He'd get the girls too and like me he had a preference for girls with big boobs. We were boob men together. On his birthday I decided I needed to get him something special. I bought him ten x-rated boob videos and I laid them out on his bed. I figured that would be a nice surprise for him when he got home. Feeling pleased with myself and the special birthday gift for Ce Ce I went out into town. The problem was that while I was out Ce Ce's mother came by the house and discovered the videos on his bed. Now Ce Ce's mom was a very religious woman, and she didn't see the funny side of it and of course Ce Ce was pretty embarrassed about it too. On another occasion she caught me in an embarrassing situation of my own. I was getting a hand job off a girl on the sofa in the front room and Ce Ce's mom just walked right in on us. And what made it even worse was that she wasn't alone. She had two of her friends from church with her too. They all yelped, 'Jesus, Jesus, Jesus!' For a while I think she looked at me like I was the fucking Devil, man.

Ce Ce has many qualities and he's a great guy to be around but he didn't have any cool. I mean he had no filter and no restraint. He just says what he's feeling and everything simply jumps out of him. His inside is his outside. Ce Ce is the kind of guy you should avoid inviting to a funeral because even if he didn't know the person, he'd be the guy crying his eyes out and making the loudest noises. The first time you ever meet Ce Ce he'll pick you right up and put you in a big bear hug. He is a man with a gigantic heart that's full of emotion.

There was a time when Ce Ce and I hung out with two other guys. They were the Fly Guys who were Guy Vaughan and Shedrick Guy. We'd go to the clubs like a band of brothers and have a great time. We got to know a beautiful girl called Dee Dee Shaw. She had a brilliant voice and Ce Ce, the Fly Guys and me also decided that we were going to write songs for her and get her a record deal. Guy wrote the first song, a really nice track called *Love is the Way to my Heart*. I wrote the next, then Ce Ce and finally Shedrick. Our band of brothers had also agreed to stay away from getting involved with her romantically because our attitude was that we shouldn't mess around with the artists in that way.

However, Guy and Ce Ce couldn't resist Dee Dee's beauty and, like I said, Ce Ce doesn't have any cool and no restraint. Both Guy and Ce Ce got into a relationship with Dee Dee. I noticed it happening and told Shedrick that we'd need to do something about it. We agreed that we needed to get Dee Dee signed before the relationships with Guy and Ce Ce came out. We agreed that I would keep Ce Ce away from Dee Dee and Shedrick would do his best to keep Guy away from her. So we had this game going on and we managed to keep it rolling for a while until one night in a club. It all came out as Ce Ce started to tell us that Dee Dee had told him that she loved him and then Guy said she had said the same to him. Guy got Dee Dee got on the phone and we are all standing around. 'Do you love me Dee Dee?' he says and she replied,

'Yeah you know I do Guy.' Next Ce Ce calls her up and says, 'Do you love me Dee Dee?' to which she replies 'Yeah sure I love you Ce Ce.' Having no cool Ce Ce yells back down the phone, 'I love you too – BITCH!' and slams the phone down. After that Ce Ce and Guy didn't write any more songs for Dee Dee and I don't think she ever got that record deal.

I first met Guy when I went to New York. There was a connection with Profile Records. That was Cory Robbins' and his label that put out a lot of hip hop artists like Run DMC. Profile asked me to do a remix on a track called *I Need Somebody* by Kechia Jenkins. Kevin Hedge from Blaze was engineering the session and it was Guy who wrote and was producing the song. The guys made me feel very welcome and I enjoyed working with them. They were very flattering too and would call me 'Marshall Genious-on'. Kechia was amazing too with an incredible vocal, I mean powerful.

That's how my friendship started with Guy and through that I met Shedrick and like I say Ce Ce, me and Guy and Shedrick would hang out in the clubs. One place we frequented was Club 88 because that was where Ce Ce and his band had a residency. That was a fun place to hang out because a lot of the football guys from the New York Giants would also be in there.

Ce Ce's band covered a lot of Luther Vandross songs. This worked for Ce Ce because he was big and fat just like Luther. I think Luther was an inspiration to many big and fat motherfuckers everywhere. Big and fat singers started to come out of the woodwork because of Luther. Prior to Luther you had to be slim and good-looking but Luther changed that. I loved Luther's stuff, he was an excellent vocalist.

I still speak to him at least once or twice a week. He is still busy and nowadays does a lot of production work. He's also involved in a group that his son plays in called Mood Life. That group was actually something that Ce Ce and me started up. When Mood Life was just Ce Ce and me we recorded an EP with Strictly Rhythm. *Needs (Not Wants)* was one of the tracks and *Work It Out* another, this track had a great vocal on it – very funky house. We recorded all the songs over at Ce Ce's house. He had a studio set up there.

Ce Ce is the best performer that I have ever seen. I mean there's plenty of people that can go and perform in a room of thousands of people and Ce Ce can do that, but you can also put Ce Ce in a room with only two people and he'll have them screaming and clapping and having the best time of their lives. The man is brilliant and, he rips it up every time.

We did the *Strictly Rhythm* EP in 1993. I remember it because I was staying at Ce Ce's house at the time. He was a New York Knicks fan and I was a Chicago Bulls fan and things would get very competitive between us. I also caused a bit of stir in his apartment too because one time, when the Bulls were playing the Knicks and the Bulls were winning, I was screaming and cheering my team on. The neighbours didn't take too kindly to this and were banging on the door yelling, 'Hey man, who you got in there screaming for the Bulls and stuff?'

I couldn't help cheering my team on. I love the Bulls and basketball. I also like the Chicago Bears, which is my football team. Things can get pretty heated in sports and between sports people. I once shared a girlfriend with one of the New York Giants. Her name was Paula. It didn't last. She was quite demanding and liked to have nice things. One time she told Ce Ce to tell me to give her some money. Apparently the football guy was giving her money and telling her to go and buy herself stuff. She and I got into a big row about this issue one night and she said, 'Marshall I ain't giving you no more pussy unless you give me some money.' This argument went on in front of Ce Ce. I simply replied, 'Well I guess I ain't getting any more pussy then' and told her to go ahead and just fuck the football guy.

Paula was a beautiful girl but she was lazy in bed. I mean after two minutes she'd have an orgasm then she didn't want to be bothered – she'd push you off. I'd imagine a big-ass professional athlete would probably pound at her for at least two hours before he was done. I think that may have happened because, sure enough, she came crawling back to me a few weeks later. I didn't give a fuck by then so I said to her, 'If you wanna get back with me, I want you to give me money, and I want fifty dollars every time you see me'.

Ce Ce and me watched a Knicks-Bulls playoff game in a strip club. The word got around that Ce Ce Rogers and Marshall Jefferson was in the joint and people were getting excited and shouting 'Everybody in the place have a good time – but not Marshall Jefferson'.

The sports culture in the US is very different to the UK but there are some similarities. At times things can get really vicious. The UK has had its own problems with the fighting at football games. How this is different to the US is that in the UK a team like Liverpool go to the game in Manchester. The two cities are not that far away. And that means the Liverpool hooligans get to meet the Manchester hooligans. So the UK has a situation where both sets of fans are at the same game. When I was living in London I would see the football fans from Chelsea or West Ham or Arsenal walking around the streets near the ground and there was trouble because the fans from both teams would run into one another. I witnessed so much hate and shit. But in the US you have situations where New York are playing Los Angeles and they are 3,500 miles away from each other, so the fans don't just turn up in numbers. This means things are a lot more peaceful and there isn't fighting in the stands.

Nowadays I think the situation has improved because generally football fans are a lot more passive. People have to be because there are consequences when the guys get arrested. And with things like cameras on phones and CCTV everywhere people can get caught much easier. The culture of sports fans has changed a lot in the last few years, back in the day you could kick somebody's ass and you didn't have to worry, but nowadays if you get caught kicking someone's ass you could end up going to prison.

Things are all messed up now in the UK anyway. I girl I knew told me that her boyfriend was going to jail for kicking some burglar's ass. What kind of shit is that when you can't even protect your own house?

Since I've been living in the UK I have missed being able to watch the Bulls and the Bears. I actually missed the last two years of the Chicago Bull's dynasty in America because I moved to the UK. They had won six championships in eight years and that was a big deal. When I go back to Chicago I do try to watch a game but it does feel strange because I'm not as familiar with the teams and the players like I used to be when I was living in Chicago and was able to see games often and follow the careers of the various players. But now I watch a Chicago Bull game and I'm, Who the fuck is that?

American DJs love sports! They love to watch games, go to games and even play sports video games. It happened in the UK too and I remember some big FIFA video game tournament that went off here in the UK. Goldie and his boys were really into that.

Goldie isn't a guy I know or can say is a friend. In fact I believe that he hates my guts. Goldie and I were at some event in New York. I walked over to him all friendly and said, 'Hi Goldie, how you doing?' He came back with a 'Don't give me all that'. I didn't understand what he meant. He told me that he used to work in some record store and one day I went in and snubbed him. Now, I don't snub anybody so I told him that I didn't snub him and if anything had happened it wasn't intentional or personal to him. But he wouldn't let it go so I just thought, oh fuck it, and walked on. He'd been carrying that grudge and he wasn't prepared to let it go.

Like I said Chicago is my home, my roots and if I had to pinpoint my favourite place to live I would have to say that house back in Chicago where I lived with Bam Bam, Mike Dunn and Sherman Burke and the other guys. I liked waking up every day and having my boys with me. We were all telling jokes all fucking day long and it was hilarious. Every day was a great day in that house.

We all laughed at Bam Bam a lot because he was so funny. He was unintentionally funny and such great fun. When I lived in Billericay he came and stayed with me for a while and we continued to laugh there too. We also played a lot of video games. One of our faves from that period was called *Age of Empires* and we played it so much that Bam Bam and me were ranked number one and two in the world. That was out of over 70,000 ranked players at the time. I actually let Bam Bam beat me for one week only so that he could be number one. I wanted him to know what it felt like to be number one. I would've let him be number one longer but he talked so much shit, I had to beat him.

I had ended up in Billericay because of a manger I had at the time. His name was Alan. When I first met Alan I was still living in Chelsea with Zeki but I needed to get out because he had met a girl and she was moving in. I could sense that a potential situation was developing. They were getting married too and he'd asked me to be the best man at his wedding. I put the word out saying that if somebody could find me a place to live before the week is out I will give them £1000.

Alan found the place and I moved out there. On my very first day I ran into some trouble with the neighbours. I also discovered the 'rules' when it came to sound systems in the UK. I was learned that the cops can come and confiscate your equipment if you get too many warnings and shit. The day I moved into my place in Billericay I was playing video games on my computer. I mean I hadn't set up my sound system at that point. I'm just happily playing my video games and I hear a knock on my door. As soon as I opened it I found myself being faced with fifteen neighbours and they looked pissed off. In fact they looked more like a lynch mob. They started complain about the noise coming from my video games and I'm just thinking wait until I've hooked up my sound system. But I took notice and that's when I moved to using headphones. Ever since my time in Billericay I've had an obsession with headphones. I must possess over forty pairs of headphones nowadays and wanting the possible sound that I can get I have some of the best headphones ever made.

My manager Alan also lived in Billericay but things didn't work out too good between us. While living in that place I spent a lot of time playing video games and I was spending £3,000 a month on them. Back then you had to pay a bill to play the games. It was still the dial-up way which meant that every time I went online I was on the clock. Also, because Bam Bam was staying with me for some of the time I had to get two lines installed. This meant there was two lines running pretty much 24/7. I didn't care especially because we were number one and number two in the world on *Age of Empires*. The thing was I wasn't aware of the bills situation because that was Alan's job to deal with.

At the time I was also working and going out for gigs and this was back in the days when I would pick up money from the gigs on the night. Nowadays I don't carry any cash from gigs. I mean DJs have been jumped over the years and robbed of their money. So I collected money from gigs and I discovered that I was also getting advances from the gigs that

I was being booked into, but Alan wasn't telling me that. Instead he was pocketing all of that advance money.

The thing was when I saw Alan after gigs he'd ask me for money taken from the gigs and he said he was using it to pay for my bills. I gave him money and thought he was paying my bills.

My mother needed something so I told Alan that I needed some money so that I could send some to Chicago. I asked him to deal with my publisher, who at that time was MCA Music. The cost to renew my publishing deal was an advance of fifty thousand pounds. I didn't see any of that because it transpired that Alan kept that for himself. He just told me that MCA weren't prepared to give me an advance.

I only found out the truth because I decided to contact MCA Music and ask them why they couldn't pay me an advance. They told me that they paid Alan £50,000. I was really pissed off with Alan and had that to that up with him. He'd also been behaving strangely and he'd trying to move me out to Croatia. While that was going on I got a summons to court for a bankruptcy hearing. I was like, What the fuck? and needed to find out what was happening. It turned out that Alan had filed for bankruptcy for me behind my back.

It turned out that Alan hadn't being paying my rent or my bills for the two years that I had been living in that place in Billericay. Alan rode around in limos all the time so I had no worries thinking my bills weren't getting paid.

When I approached Alan about all this shit that he had brought to my door and asked me why my rent and bills hadn't been paid he said, 'It's because I hate you'. I was really surprised. I had no idea what was going on with him. I mean he had bought me Christmas presents and stuff. I now know it was with my own money, but at the time I just thought he was being a good guy.

I asked him why he hated me and said what have I ever done to you? He replied what have you ever done for me? It was all very strange and unexpected. I mean I had been giving him twenty per cent of everything that I had earned. I was very shocked by it all and our relationship ended there. Well, actually it ended in court.

I went to court and I explained to them that I hadn't been paying my rent and bills because the understanding I had was that my manager was taking care of that stuff. I told them that I was giving Alan money every month and presumed everything was being dealt with. I told the judge the whole story about Alan keeping the advance monies from gig bookings and MCA and the judge basically told me he was dismissing the bankruptcy and told me to get out of his court.

The stupid part was that some years later Alan called me up. He called me right out of the blue and was all friendly and shit and he said stuff like 'They were good times we had weren't they?' I just sat there thinking 'What the fuck?' and ended our conversation.

I left Billericay and went back to living in London. I had become friends with a guy called Andy Grober. Andy played guitar, worked in music publishing and also had a connection with Thin Lizzy from their very early days. Andy got involved in collecting some of my publishing money on my behalf, which really helped.

Andy's place was in Battersea which wasn't that far away from where I had been living in Chelsea, but it was very different. I have many fond memories of living with Andy. We had a lot of fun. He'd sit around and play guitar and we'd talk about rock music and bands like Thin Lizzy. We appreciated a lot of the same bands so could spend hours just chatting about them. It was like being back in Chicago when I was growing up and discovering bands like Led Zeppelin and Black Sabbath all over again.

Andy had lots of rock and roll stories which I liked to listen to. He told me about the times he'd hung out with The Who and getting into a car with Keith Moon but Keith commanding his driver to stop the car because he wanted to drive. The driver protested because he knew Keith had a habit of wrecking his cars.

I liked hearing stories about Keith Moon because I loved Keith's drumming. How can you not love anyone who drums with so much energy? I would have liked to have seen The Who but I didn't really get properly into them until the 2000s. I loved Tommy though. I had the video of that and must have played it at least forty times. Tina Turner the Acid Queen, ooh man!

After living with Andy with a while I met a girl. She was also a Scientologist. Her name was Rachael. Rachael had a place in Chiswick and her roommate moved out so I ended up moving in. I had known Rachael in the 1990s but we had lost touch and somehow we found each other again in the 2000s and we started up a relationship.

So I was with Rachael and we're living together and all was good, but then she fell pregnant. Things were about to change. She worked as a nanny but did that for some high profile people. Paul McCartney was one of her clients. Being a nanny was what she did and loved and it paid well and faced with the prospect of having her own kid kind of threw her and she started to unravel.

Something in Rachael changed. She started to tell me that she wanted us to get a bigger house in a better area. But she wanted to live in the rich parts of London like Chelsea and be around the wealthy people. I knew it wasn't possible and besides, Chiswick was a very nice area and the rent a lot cheaper than anywhere in Chelsea.

Her moods were hard to live with and she had moods 24/7. It got that bad that we agreed to go and have couples counselling via the Church of Scientology. Rachael seemed to think to the church would jump on her side because she considered herself the full-time Scientologist and I was just a casual member.

We both gave our accounts of how we felt things were going and after the counsellor heard our stories she pretty much said, 'Bitch, you're crazy, this is a good man – get out!' Of course those exact words weren't used but that's what I heard. In the end Rachael didn't have the baby and we went our separate ways. I couldn't run fast enough out of that door.

I next went to live in the Baker Street area of London. I stayed in a hotel there for a good year. I briefly got back with Rachael but it didn't last. I then moved to Manchester.

There was a contest and I was the prize. It was a DJ contest and the winner got to have a record co-produced with me. The guy who won was called James Fennings and he invited me to Manchester because his mother was going to cook dinner. I got introduced to his brother Phil too. I went to Phil's house and he had a huge place. I asked him how much the rent was and he told me it was £700. I thought that was brilliant especially as I was paying more than double that back in London and I was getting much smaller places. So I thought fuck it, I'll move to Manchester.

It turned out that Phil needed a flatmate so I moved into his place. I ended up living with Phil for ten years. During that time we had various places around Manchester. One of those places was in an area called Ramsbottom, which was an old market town located in the Greater Manchester area. People joke saying it's the place where the men are mean and the sheep are scared.

I've been living in Manchester for a long time now and I love the city. I like the people and have made friends here. I currently live in the Prestwich area where there's a big Jewish community. I believe it's the second biggest Jewish community outside of London. At first the locals were unsure about me but as they've got to know me they have warmed to me and we talk. They are forever giving me advice, so I guess I must appear to them as being a little stupid.

When I get downtime I liked to venture out to Printworks. That's where the cinema is and a bunch of bars and restaurants. The Arndale is a good place to go shopping as is the Trafford Centre. Eastern Bloc Records is another place I will visit. I had played in the shop a few times. It rains a lot in Manchester but I don't care because I stay inside most of the time, just playing video games and talking to my friends and family on the phone.

I'm fortunate to have a lot of family and friends who look out for me. They showed their concern on the day of the Manchester Arena bombing on May 22nd 2017. That was when a twenty-two-year-old terrorist attacked those kids at the Ariana Grande concert. Twenty-three were killed and over a hundred injured in the blast. I got a lot of calls from the States asking if I was okay. They were shocked, I was shocked. Manchester was shocked but what surprised me was that the people of Manchester were sort of upbeat and defiant about what had happened. There was a spirit that showed the terrorists that they hadn't won. The people of Manchester united and showed the world their strength. I guess that helped a lot of people that had been directly affected by the tragic event in some ways. What I observed in the people of Manchester was an attitude that said, 'Fuck you, we have our way of life and we're going to fight to keep it.' The people of Manchester bounced back from the IRA bombing of their city in 1996, so I guess they knew they could bounce back again.

The other significant terrorist attack in recent years was the World Trade Centre. When those planes that had been taken over by members of al-Qaeda flew into the Twin Towers on September 11th 2001, killing near three thousand people and injuring thousands more, the world got shaken up – myself included.

At the time I was at an event in London. People gathered around a TV and watched what was happening. People just didn't know what to make of what they were witnessing. Nobody had any reference points in themselves to help them to understand what they were seeing. I was stood with them thinking to myself, 'What the fuck is going on here?'

While I watched the TV people were saying to me stuff like 'Sorry to see what's happening Marshall'. They did this because they knew that I was American. I struggled to understand what was going on. I also had a lot of friends in New York and I was worried about them. Fortunately none of the people I knew that lived in New York were harmed in the attack.

When things happen of a terrorist nature of course it affects me, but it doesn't really hit home. The thing is I have lived in some really hard areas in Chicago, where when you walk down the street, you worry that someone might shoot you. When I lived in those sorts of places the threat of getting shot was an everyday occurrence. The threat of getting bombed by a terrorist seems kind of far away to me.

I'm sure my friends in New York felt the after affects of the attack on their city, despite a lot of those guys growing up in tough areas like I had back in Chicago.

When I lived in Inglewood in Chicago I really did worry about dying. When I walk down the street here in Manchester I don't worry about dying. I certainly don't worry about getting blown up by some terrorist.

When I lived in those tough places in Chicago people were getting killed by stray bullets and all they were doing were strolling down to the grocery store. When you live in hard neighbourhoods you learn to live with more immediate fears. When you live in tough streets you put thoughts of terrorist attacks away in the back of your mind because your concerns are about the guy who is walking towards you.

When I lived in that house with Bam Bam and my boys that was located in the heart of the ghetto and, even though we knew everybody, it still didn't stop us getting robbed. Getting our stuff robbed was bad but it could have been a lot worse for anyone of us. We could have got killed. For instance Fast Eddie knew everybody in his neighbourhood but he got robbed at gunpoint. My friend Gershon Jackson, who also lived in that house with Bam Bam and me, had a tragic incident concerning his family. Some guys broke into his brother's house at Christmas time and killed him and his wife and kids. Gershon was supposed to go over to his brother's place on that fateful day but something prevented him going and so he stayed home. If he'd gone he too would have probably been killed.

Another friend of mine Reggie Hall, who was another guy who loved with Bam Bam, Gershon and me, got shot and almost died. Due to his injuries he can hardly walk now. I remember Reggie was in a club in a bad neighbourhood and he had a bullet fly by him and scrape the top of his head. It was that close. That wasn't even a bullet meant for him. The guy who shot that gun was aiming for someone else and Reggie just happened to be sitting in the wrong place. This is the kinda shit that happens in the ghettos.

Gang violence is as problematic today in the neighbourhoods of Chicago as it was when I was a kid, if anything worse because there is no gang unity in Chicago. Kids in gangs are getting shot and messed up way too often and, what is worse, kids who are not gang-related are getting killed by stray bullets fired by the kids affiliated with gangs. That sort of thing is happening every day but because it's so frequent nobody cares about it. I heard that there have been more gang-related killings in Chicago in the last decade than what there has been in Afghanistan in the same period.

This is the kid of immediate worries that I'm talking about. People walking around their neighbourhoods have more pressing concerns about stray bullets and gangs than some terrorist kid with a bomb tucked in his back pack.

A rapper I know called IRoc T who Mike Dunn produced got shot five times in the head. This wasn't a gang-related murder though. I heard that he had been playing dice with some drug dealers and, because he was winning loads of games, the dealers accused him of having a loaded dice. Now, I knew Trav and he was just a lucky guy and so I doubt he needed to cheat at dice.

I've had guns pulled on me twice in my lifetime. The first time it happened I hadn't long turned fourteen years' old. At the time I was in one of the bathrooms at high school. I was simply minding my own business and taking care of business and the next thing I know some guy is pushing a gun into my back. There wasn't much I could do except listen to the guy's demands. He basically said 'Give me all your money or I'm going to shoot you'. There was another guy in the bathroom too and he pipes up in my defence and says 'Hey let him be man, he's just a sophomore', which meant that I was a second year student. I think the guy with the gun was actually searching for freshmen. I guess he expected them to have more money or would be intimidated easily. Once the gunman learned that I was a sophomore he let me go and I exited the bathroom as fast as my legs would carry me.

The other time I came into contact with a gun was when I was about twenty-three years old. I was in a club in Chicago and it was back in the days when I was drinking and getting high too. At the time my girlfriend Esther and me had split up. It was one of our brief periods of being apart around that time. I was in the club, having fun and a girl caught my eye. Well, I ended up getting close to her and we stared to flirt with each other. At some point in the night I walked outside to get some fresh air. I was on my own and just minding my own business. Suddenly this dude came up to me, pulls out a gun and sticks it right in my face.

I held my hands up as if to say 'Hey man, what's going on?' and the dude says 'What you doing? You're fucking around with Pretty Tony's girl'. Before he had time to speak again something in me clicked into survival mode and I grabbed the gun off of him and pushed him away. But I reckon my survival instinct wasn't satisfied with just pushing this guy away so the next thing I know I'm beating down on the guy with his own gun. And man, I really did beat his ass as I'm screeching at him 'Yeah, you can tell Pretty Tony this is what happens when you mess with me!'

After I beat up that dude I walked off with his gun and I jumped into my car, which was parked quite near the club. I calmly drove away so as to not attract any more attention to myself. About a mile down the road I tossed the gun out of the window and just drove on and tried to put the incident out of my mind.

Trying to live a life and stay alive in the ghetto is a challenge and if it's not the gangs trying to get you it may be the cops. For a black kid the cop can still be a problem. As recent as 2018 I was with Victor Romeo, the guy who did *Love Will Find a Way* and *Inside You,* and riding around Chicago in a car with a girl who Victor knew. She was a firearms instructor and her job included certifying people who had guns who can conceal and carry.

As we were driving around she was telling us about the laws relating to conceal and carry and stuff like that and then all of a sudden she says 'Oh shit'. We asked her what was up and she told us that we were being followed by cops. Victor and I weren't concerned. I mean, nobody was carrying any weed or anything. As far as we were concerned we weren't doing anything wrong but she told us that the police were following her. I asked her why and she explained that the police had probably ran her plates and checked her history out and found out that she was connected to guns. She also told us that, despite her being a legal gun owner, this wasn't something that the cops like. She said the cops just don't like black people carrying guns around. As soon as she said that I started to think, shit. I started to worry because there I was driving around Chicago with another big black motherfucker and a black female and the cops know someone in the car is carrying a gun. I guess some things haven't changed since my dad was cop and left after hearing white cops bragging about killing a black guy. My dad had just too much dignity to stick around with stuff like that.

Over the years there have been just too many stories of killings and robbings and I know DJs that have run into trouble too. Thankfully there aren't too many stories of DJs getting robbed or mugged at gigs but it has happened. It's always a risk having to deal with large sums of money and a lot of DJs get paid on the night of their gig, so this means they are carrying their earnings and people know this.

I'm very careful when it comes to my wages from playing a set. These days I don't carry cash at all. When I leave a club after playing my set I'm not carrying money. That's just stupid. Any money I have made would have been transferred to my bank account already. You have to remember I have spent thirty years travelling to countries that I know virtually nothing about. I don't know the people, the rules, the way their crimes are committed. But I'll be in one of their clubs and everybody in the club knows I'm getting paid for being there and they're probably thinking that before I leave the club the promoter is going to pay me in cash and it's going to be a significant amount of money too. I understand this so I tell the promoter that I want to be paid before I get on that plane.

Fast Eddie has had some bad luck. When he lived two doors away from my house he ran into some trouble. This was on the West Side of Chicago, which was a really rough area. It's stupid really and sometimes I think on it, but I came up in a good neighbourhood with a caring and loving family, that kept us all safe and then I moved to the ghetto. I can't recall why I moved to live in that area with Fast Eddie, I had enough money to be able to live some place else. So Fast Eddie got into some trouble at the time when he was big and everybody knew him and knew he was getting paid well. He got robbed at gunpoint. A bunch of guys came to his home and stuck a gun to his head. Fast Eddie was fortunate to get out of that situation with his life.

Another guy I knew went to buy a drum machine. He had four thousand dollars on him and some guy intercepted him and robbed him at gunpoint. The bad guys have a way of figuring out who has money and what they are intending to do and I'm always thinking about this stuff. I'm very cautious and I'm very careful not to reveal too much inside information about my movements and intentions. It's not a matter of being paranoid, I'm just drawing on my experience of having seen so many other DJs getting robbed.

I also have a lot of friends who I don't really hang out with back in Chicago because they're crack heads. It's nothing personal but you just have shit that they want and when they know I'm back in Chicago they call me up and they want to hang out, but I know they want my money so they can go and buy more crack. I get really offended when they call me up and ask me questions like what time will I be in this place or that area. I don't like people timing my movements in Chicago because you cannot always trust people. I don't have this issue in the UK. In the UK I'll tell you where I'm going to be and what time and I'll even show up early. This is what I'm talking about, this stuff is close to me – the terrorist stuff just isn't.

CHAPTER THIRTEEN

Marshall is so iconic regarding what he has done. As a producer I credit him as the Godfather of House Music, without a shadow of a doubt. I know there was Frankie Knuckles too but you had a man like Marshall working with people like Ten City and Ce Ce Rogers and the music that Marshall made with them was the cornerstone of House music as we know it today. The music that Marshall was able to create, in the mid to late 80s, was made at a slightly more developed level than what had gone previously. House music before Marshall was much more basic, but Marshall did was take it to a whole new level and because of tracks like Move Your Body, *he helped House music gain momentum.*

From a DJ's perspective like myself, Frankie was there first and he was a DJ, but it was Marshall who was the producer first. I think Marshall's career as a DJ came later as a way to support his producing career. Marshall's songs have stood the test of time because they are songs. Marshall has never made a throw-away club record.

The Ten City album Foundation *changed my life. I can put my hand on my heart and say that that is one of the best albums I have ever, ever heard. Up until that album I wasn't really into dance music at all. I was into hip hop and soul. But that Ten City album was a transition for me from soulful music and electronic music. I completely got it and everything changed for me after that. We are missing the Marshall Jeffersons in the industry right now. He was in every sense of the word a record producer and using a drum machine and a sequencer he made songs. Marshall's music has probably influenced much more than I know. Yeah, I look to Marshall as being the Godfather of House.*

Mark Knight

The 2000s was a new era for House and dance music. Y2K didn't happen so we all just partied on from January 1st and everybody's computers continued to work and the world didn't implode.

The Ultra Music Festival in Miami started up around that time and this ran alongside the Winter Music Conference (WMC), which had been going since the mid 80s. The two festivals were connected at various times and I believe since 2018 the WMC has been taken over by the Ultra Music Festival.

I attended one of the early WMCs. There were a lot of people from the industry present and a lot of people trying their best to get deals. But I don't recall seeing much business being done, what I saw was a lot partying and that seemed to be the emphasis. It was nothing like the New Music Seminar in New York or the Amsterdam Dance Event, which had a strong focus on business.

These sort of events all started up around the late 90s and early 2000s and were intended to promote new artists from the electronic dance music world. What was certain was the dance music wasn't going away and it was a growing industry. Going into the 2000s I think dance music got more polished. I think it became more formulaic too because the various genres were now defined. This in turn meant that many people just ran with whatever genre they were aligned to and I think this was kind of restricting.

In the 2000s there also seemed to be a lot of promotional videos being made with pretty girls wearing very little clothing. It was as if dance music caught up with rap. Sex was being used to sell House music to the masses. Now videos cost a lot of money to make; I mean you have to pay the production team, editors, the models and in the 2000s record labels had the money to throw at the artists to have their videos made. Videos are a way to reach lots and lots of people and videos with pretty girls washing sports cars or dancing around swimming pools with cocktail glasses in their hands are a sure way to get people's attention. This period of getting budgets eventually dried up on the scale that it had been on because the market got flooded, and sales for some of the songs wasn't high enough.

While all the seminars and videos were going on I continued to do my thing and in 2001 I got together with DJ Pierre to do a track called *Everybody Dance (Clap Your Hands)*. Like myself DJ Pierre had continued to make House music since parting company with Trax Records and throughout the 90s. Like myself he'd also put records out with

Strictly Rhythm. It had been a long time since DJ Pierre and I had worked on Acid Tracks. It was a lot of fun working with him on the *Everybody Dance* track and we also got in a vocalist called Janine Cross to perform on the track.

DJ Pierre set the whole project up and he had his own label DJP which stood for DJ Pierre. DJ Pierre and I simply got together in the studio and we hung out and messed around and we came up with the song. We actually recorded the track in a studio in Essex because for some reason DJ Pierre was in the UK.

Music Makes Me Happy was the next song that got released. The A-side was the *Rich Bitch Vocal Mix* and the B-side the *Da Beatmunger Mix*. The song came out on Cleveland City Records. It was a good feel record with the lyrics 'You make me so very happy, I'm so glad I found you'. JD Braithwaite provided the main vocals. The song was actually a sample from a song that we'd done back 1994 called *I Found You*. The essence of the song is contained in the lyrics 'Music is my life, it's the only way' and that has meaning for a lot of people.

My next release was *69%* which I did with Serge Imhof. Serge was a DJ from Switzerland and he wanted to do a song with me. I speak over the music. I'm recounting a conversation I had with Serge about the meaning of 69%. Serge told me the meaning of 69%, 'That's just the way it is –70% is too much, 68% you owe me one, so it must be 69%'. So *69%*. The whole percentage thing was actually something that I got from Sherman Burke back in Chicago because he would brag about not going down on women. He'd say, 'I don't do sixty-nine, I do sixty-eight, so that's where you do me and I owe you one'. So I took that and cleaned it up on the track with Serge.

I go on to describe how the music is starting to move my body. My right leg starts to move first, then it's my left and then it builds up until my head is moving and 'I'm locked into the groove' just like any funky House song should make you do.

Serge lived in Zurich. I remember the first time that I played there. I was in a club and this girl came right up to me and started to kiss me. We wound up hooking up for the night and had a pretty cool time together. It lasted for a while because we were having so much fun. She always seemed to have a lot of money with her too and sometimes she'd fly to the UK to see me and there were other times when I'd fly to Zurich to see her.

During one of our hooking-up times I decided to ask her how it was that she had so much money. I wanted to find out what she did for a living. She told me that she was a dominatrix and that it paid well. Well, I thought on this for a while and talked to Zeki about her and we came to the conclusion that she was basically a hooker. I asked her about it and she broke down and admitted that she was a hooker and asked me not to think any differently about her. Things were different though and I stuck it out for a few more months. Then the pretty white girl with long black hair, with a sensational body that I had been hanging out, with gave me VD and that was the last straw.

Coffee To Go was a track released under Fuf and Goz on Kinky Vinyl.

I recorded the song in Croatia. It was my manager Alan who came up with the name Fuf and Goz but I have no idea what it means. It was just me on the track. I wrote and produced and played all the instruments on the instrumental. I believe Alan played around with it later on and he did a very nice of it too. Kinky Vinyl was linked to Whoop! Records who were a London-based label. They put records out by Nathan G who also did a mix of *Coffee To Go*.

I didn't put any records out for a couple of years. I was just busy travelling around the world playing in clubs, hooking up with my friends and family back in Chicago and kicking back with video games. My next release wasn't until 2005. That was a song called *Feel Me* and I got Rachael Pearson to feature on. For this track I went back to adding a piano that was close to the *Move Your Body* style. Rachael was my girlfriend that I mentioned although she wasn't my girlfriend at the time when we did the song. The studio session was pretty smooth and the song came together easily enough and Rachael was able to lay down her vocals with very little effort. She had a sweet voice that suited the feel of the song. After we had done the song we went our separate ways and it was a few months until we met each other again. If I remember correctly we hooked up in Piccadilly Circus, London and went to see a movie together. Things just kind of developed from there.

Feel Me was put out by USB Records. This was a label set up in 2005 by me Ce Ce Rogers and David Dee. USB stood for Universal Soul Brothers and during the labels lifetime we put out records like Ce Ce's *Beautiful*, Moodlife's *Call Me* and a track by Paris Brightledge, the guy that had sung the vocals on *It's All Right*, the song I had all the trouble over with Sterling Void almost twenty years earlier.

David Dee was a DJ from Malta. He played a big part in running the label and doing the promotion on the various records that USB put out. Most of the music that was put out by USB was done by Ce Ce and me and much of the music that was written was made in Ce Ce's studio back in New Jersey.

The *Colours* EP was also put out on USB. I recorded the tracks in Chicago. There were four instrumentals included on the EP and each had a title of a particular colour. The colours were meant to describe moods as I felt them. There was green which reminded me of the forest, there was blue which represented the moody thing, there was brown which I liked to funk – anything that had that feel of James Brown and then there was orange which simply reminded me of a sunny day.

It didn't take too long to write and record the tracks. I think no longer than a week. I played everything on the songs. It was just me, all me making music in the studio.

There was a few years' break before anything else connected to me was released and when it did it was a remix of *Raindance* which was a song I had done under Ragtyme along with Byron Stingily. It had been almost twenty-five years since we had first written and recorded that stuff. It was a popular song back then and Ten City would often perform it at their shows. The remixed version was put out by Z Records which was a label run by Dave Lee and Joey Negro. They had some good artists on the label, people like Jakatta and Raven Maize.

I don't know if *Raindance* inspired some UK rave promoters but in 1989 a team of Londoners started putting on parties called Raindance. They held some big parties in a venue in Jenkins Lane, East London and continued for a few years and in more recent years have started to put raves back on.

Those three years between *Colours* and *Raindance* were hard to make any money from making music. I would get approached about doing this or doing that but it was tough for me to visualize making anything from it. I don't like dragging my friends into some project that I don't think is going to make them any money. I just don't do that. This is my present situation. I'm not writing or releasing any songs because it's hard to see them making any money. I just don't make music and put it out and hope that it'll make money – this isn't the way that I go about things. Even back in the days when I was doing *Move Your Body* I knew I had to get the record pressed up because I knew it would make money. I knew it would be in demand. And *Move Your Body* did make some money and whatever money it made I split it with the other guys.

In the 80s and the 90s it was easy to see how my music was going to make money, but in the 2000s there was so much music being made, it was hard to see how any money was going to be made. This became a problem and that was partly why I ended up making records like *Colours* that was just me. I did that because I didn't want to get other guys involved that I knew I couldn't pay.

What I did do in the 2000s was release compilation albums. The first was called *Welcome to the World of Marshall Jefferson*. This was a double CD with a subtitle *A Testament to House Music*. CD 1 was called *The Beginning* 'a historic testament to the creation of house music, featuring the classics that have shaped the house sound of today'. For that I selected a bunch of songs that I felt represented the purpose of the album. I included songs such as Bam Bam's *Give It To Me* and Alison Limerick's *Where Love Is*. There were also some tracks from me: *Move Your Body* and *The Cow*. The second side was titled Marshall Jefferson 2001 'the electrifying sound of Marshall Jefferson in the new millennium featuring a selection of the latest dance floor anthems and unreleased material'. I included the Noosa Heads *Mushrooms* track alongside *Gotta Thing* by the Foreal People and *Finally* from Kings of Tomorrow. The CD also came with a CD ROM of an exclusive interview with myself.

In 2003 I was approached again to do another compilation and that was *Move Your Body: The Evolution of Chicago House*. This was done with a guy called Ian Dewhirst and as the sleeve notes stated the songs on the album were meant to 'accurately represent the original house music scene from the mid 1980s to the early 1990s. Also in the sleeve notes I wrote a few words about what the songs meant to me. For example on the album I included *Don't Make Me Wait* by the Peech Boys and I explained how it wasn't considered to be a typical House record but that it was huge. There was also Ce Ce's *Someday*, Joe Smooth's *Promised Land*, Phuture's *Acid Tracks*, Ten City's *Devotion* and Jungle Wonz's *Time Marches On*. There was also *I Can't Turn Around* by Isaac Hayes. This was the jam that Farley 'Jackmaster' Funk made into *Love Can't Turn Around*.

This compilation was really just a collection of hits that I recognised from those days back in the clubs in Chicago. Mixing the tracks only took an afternoon. I mean it's not rocket science – it's just deejaying.

The following year the guys from Salsoul contacted me wanting me to do a compilation album for them. That was *My Salsoul* Marshall Jefferson presents *The Foundations Of House*. The songs on that compilation were what we listened to back in the days that formed the basis for House music because all of this stuff was what Frankie Knuckles and Ron Hardy was playing.

Salsoul was street talk of the Latinos which combined soul music and salsa music. The label had started up in the mid 70s and the label used many of session musicians from the 'Philly sound'. It was the 70s disco influence mixed with big orchestras. Salsoul kind of refined the Philly sound.

Earl Young was one of the main guys that helped to create that Salsoul/Philly sound. He was the drummer. Earl was from Philadelphia and is credited as being the guy responsible for creating that disco-style drumming. He used the hi-hat in a way that drummers weren't doing at that time and he laid the template for a style that grew and grew and was very influential for House music. Earl also founded The Trammps who had a huge hit with *Disco Inferno*. When we did the Ten City album we got Earl Young in to play the drums.

The *My Salsoul* album also included tracks like *Jingo-Candido*, *Just As Long As I Got You* – Love Committee, *Double Cross* – First Choice and *Let No Man Put Asunder* which was a huge hit for First Choice. Salsoul was responsible for so much great music. This was the stuff that I was playing when I was first going out as a DJ.

On *Foundations Of House* I also included Loleatta Holloway's *Love Sensation*. This was the song that Black Box sampled for their track *Ride On Time*, which was a number one hit in the UK in 1989. When the song was released they didn't credit Loleatta Holloway for her vocals and it became a legal issue, which resulted in Black Box having to settle an undisclosed sum to the original people who did the song. When I first heard *Ride On Time* I thought, 'Oh shit, another rip-off.' That was my attitude. I saw a great song being ripped off. I wasn't keen on the Black Box song at all. It bothers me too to think that the guys who did the original version had paid out an entire orchestra, session musicians and studio time and then some kid comes along and samples their hard work. I can't get past the whole sampling thing. Some people can but I just can't. I've been sampled so much I know how it feels. I tolerate people sampling my music but I don't like it.

It's nice to be asked to put together compilation albums but it doesn't take that much work. It's not like making a record. When you put together a compilation album you just pick out the hits that you like, but when you make a record you have to use other senses and you have to put your heart and soul into it. When you deejay you're just playing a record and it doesn't matter how tired you are or how sick you are, that record will just carry on playing. You can be up there dying of a heart attack and the record will continue to jam its ass off.

CHAPTER FOURTEEN

Marshall's music danced into my life in 1986. It's now 2019 and he's still there and his music continues to sound amazing. I chose Let's Get Busy *as the theme music to my show on Centreforce Radio because of its energy and vitality and, the way it puts a huge smiley face on me every time – but then all of Marshall's songs do that to me. I feel fortunate to say that Marshall is now my friend and my world is the better for it.*

Ian 'Snowy' Snowball

In 2009 Fabio Tosti released *Mind and Soul*. This was a song that sampled my music. I had released *Marshall Jefferson House Generation* because of the sampling issue. This was a collection of samples that I was making available to producers and DJs and it was put out with loopmasters.

I got together a few guys to help put together *House Generation*: Sherman Burks, Paris Brightledge, Byron Stingily and Orbit Davis from the Chicago Jazz Philharmonic, who helped to capture strings and brass.

The idea behind *House Generation* was that I would make a specific collection of music that was intended for people to sample. This meant that there was a large selection of new material that people could buy and then they didn't need to sample from my already released songs like *Move Your Body*. I ended up doing two volumes of *House Generation*. People were then free to use my samples but they were not free to use my name unless I approved it. Fabio bugged me for so long that I thought, 'Oh fuck it, go ahead' and I gave him permission to sample me and credit me on *Mind and Soul*.

It was towards the end of the decade that I got back together with my girlfriend Shelia. I'm still with her now. Shelia and I had first got together in the 90s. I knew her brother and he'd invited me to a party. His brother had a girlfriend and she was Vicky Ryan the singer that I had worked with. The party was to celebrate Vicky getting her huge record deal. The party was in Long Branch New Jersey where he lived. I wasn't actually that keen on going to the party because I had had enough of partying by the mid 90s. But I did go and I knocked on the door and this girl answered it and let me in. That girl had a gigantic cleavage which meant that I didn't see anything else for the rest if the night. The party was full of beautiful women and I was told that I could have any girl there. Well, I didn't have to think too much on it and said, well, I want the girl that answered the door. I was met with 'That's my sister – you want her?' and so Sheila turned out to be the sister of the guy that had invited me to the party. And that was how Sheila and I got together.

Sheila and I stayed in a relationship for a few years following that party. We had our ups and we had our downs. The thing was Sheila wanted to get married. That's what she wanted but getting married wasn't something that I wanted. Every time we broke up it was because of the marriage issue.

After one break-up we didn't talk for a period and then she called me up one day to tell me that she was engaged to be married to some guy. He's name was Rick and they'd had a relationship when they were kids. I listened to what she told me and I congratulated her on her engagement. I mean Rick sounded like a really nice guy and she was getting what she wanted, which to be married.

The next thing I know Sheila's in Chicago and she's telling me that the wedding is off. We got back together and had another go at our relationship. After a few months the marriage issue came up again and we broke up again because I still didn't want to get married. Sheila found another guy and got she got engaged again, but that fell through and we got back together again.

The marriage thing kind of went quiet for a while but then Shelia told me that she wanted to have kids. But I didn't want kids either. I just didn't want to get married and I just didn't want to have kids. We broke up again but then we got back together and this time Sheila told me that she wouldn't mention the whole marriage or kids thing again.

Well, Sheila did mention marriage again and we broke up. There was then a period where we didn't speak. She'd try calling me but I wouldn't pick up. She got a new guy and she did get married and she had two kids Esor and Talia. Shelia's marriage didn't work out though and we ended up getting back together and this is our present situation. I get along pretty well with the kids and we all see each other often. They live in the States. Sheila also comes to spend the summer with me.

The marriage thing came up again. Sheila asked for a ring, just something that signified our relationship. But I told her that I wasn't going to get her a ring. However, I was on Facebook and I'm flirting with an ex-girlfriend and Sheila saw this. I was just flirting. Nothing was going to happen but I'm in the dog house. I mean, I'm fucked! But what Sheila told me was that she'd forget about it if I got her a ring. I told her that I didn't want to get her a ring but if I did, how could that possibly erase what is in her mind about me flirting with some ex-girlfriend who I had been with thirty years earlier? She told me it would and you know what? I got her that ring.

The two kids are great and I'm glad that we all get along. Sheila is great with them too. She's a really good mom. In fact she's turned into the world's greatest mother. She does a lot for them and one time put a party on for them which I was asked to go and help out with.

The party was at her house and thirty of those little fuckers came and took over the place. I asked Sheila what time they were leaving and she said ten thirty. I said that was good, ten thirty and they will be getting the fuck out of there. Within the first thirty minutes I got banished from the party. The thing was all these kids are like thirteen years old and I know what I was like when I was that age and I didn't want anything to go down. I guess Sheila didn't like the way I was monitoring the situation. She told me that I was making everybody nervous and nobody wants to dance with me around. I said, What kind of dancing do they want to do then that doesn't involve me being around? But I got told to go upstairs and stay away from the party. I went to the bedroom and fell asleep.

I woke up at midnight, got my shit together and went downstairs and all the little motherfuckers are still in the house and the party is still going on. I went to find Sheila and ask why all the kids are still in the house and she replies telling me that she'd allowing them all to spend the night. I yelled 'Spending the night?' which meant I fucked up again. But I did take control of the situation and I told all the boys to sleep in one area and all the girls to sleep in another. Thirty of them, right? It was chaos.

It had been three years since the re-release of *Raindance* and I was due to put something out. *We Groove U* by Harley and Muscle was released in 2011 on Soulstar Records. Peter Cataldo is Harley and Falvio Romaniello is Muscle. They are based in Milan, Italy. I've known those guys for a long time and we got together to make the song. They did the music and I did the vocals. I'm talking on the record, saying stuff like 'we groove u university' and I explain that I'm the 'professor of houseology' and I also say that 'house music can be found in the afterlife' and 'house music can be found anywhere that you go'.

Harley and Muscles recorded the song in Italy and they sent me the music. I then recorded the vocals in the New Jersey. It's a way music can be made nowadays.

I had got to know Harley and Muscles because they'd come to see me when I played in Italy and I have been to Italy a lot of times. They kind of helped me out too when it's been time to deal with the business side of things. In my experience the Italians can sometimes be a bit dodgy. Some of those guys don't like to pay you at the end of the night. A few times Flavio has stepped in to make sure that I got paid. It was because of my experiences of having trouble getting paid that I now have the policy of getting paid before I get on that plane.

I've had Italian booking agents over the years and one was Francesca. She'd get me with the sound of her voice every time. She'd call me up and say 'Marrrsshall, when do you come to etaly?' I love the Italians and I had an Italian girlfriend for a time and she was talking to me in that sexy Italian way. She'd call me up and also say 'Marrrsshall, when do you come to etaly?' and I would reply 'Well, it's going to be another six months until I'm next in Italy'. She'd come back with 'Six-a-months? No Marrrsshall, that-a-too long, why you make me wait? I wait for you'.

I like Italy a lot. Naples is a great place to party. I've had some really good parties in Italy. There was place I played, I can't remember where it was now but it was snowing at the time and such was the snowstorm that nobody turned out. But I was there and I'm looking at an almost empty room. The owner of the place came and found me and said 'Okay, here's what we're going to do, we're going to have a private party'. I said 'okay' and then he points to the DJ booth and says 'You play on the left turntable and that black-haired girl will sucka yer dick and if you play on the right turntable the brunette girl will sucka yer dick'.

I wasn't expecting that and I think for a moment and check out the two girls. But I also didn't want to pull out my dick in front of the people in the place. I look at the owner, right in his eyes and I say 'I'm insulted'. He looks stunned. I then say 'Look man, I'm a master mixer' and I point to the DJ booth and the girls and continue with 'I always play two decks at the same time'. It took the owner a moment to understand but he got there and started to laugh.

Italy is a beautiful country with lots of old stuff too. They stick to their own language too and hardly any of them speak English. You go to a restaurant and they don't understand you so they tell you to wait while they go and get someone who they say 'Speaks a good English' but all they do is return with another no-English-speaking motherfucker. But I get it and it's my fault for not being able to speak Italian in their home.

The food is fantastic in Italy too. Pasta/pizza is Italy. They've got a lot of good shit in Italy. The only problem is that since they've become part of the European Union they've been putting preservatives in their food and that detracts from the quality and taste of their wonderful food.

Nowadays whenever I got to Italy I tell them that the best pasta/pizza I've ever had was in Croatia. They always tell me to get the fuck out, but it's the truth. There are a lot of Italians in Croatia and they make their pasta/pizza better than the guys still living back home. In Croatia they grow much of their own food and the vegetables are bursting with flavour. Everything is so fresh because they're not fucking their food up with preservatives.

However, having said that there is one cool place in Italy that I do like to go that does make excellent food. That place was in Naples and the English translation of the place's name comes out as my mother's kitchen. It's only a small place with no more than eight seats. Their pasta/pizza was so good it almost made me cry.

Food is a wonderful thing and because I have travelled the world I have been privileged to sample so many foods. I've had the best sausages and the best pasta/pizza, but when I'm home I like to make salads. A salad would be my signature dish and that's boring. But I like to make salads with cucumbers, tomatoes, black olives, calamari, avocados and onions. Also because of where I live in the Jewish area of Manchester I get the foods I need to make what they call an Israeli salad, but I do my own version of it.

To top off the salads I make my own salad dressing. I'll share with you my secret ingredients. I use ginger (root not powder), turmeric, oil and instead of vinegar I use limes. I then add some grapes to sweeten it. Next I toss in some pepper corns and chillies and blend it all together. Sometimes I might put in some coriander leaves or garlic cloves too, and I have my salad dressing to put onto my salad and that is a fine meal.

CHAPTER FIFTEEN

Marshall Jefferson was the first person I bought on Trax.
Move Your Body *was one of the first house records that I got
and played in Flicks in 1986 and it always got people on the
dance floor. Flicks was really a soul and funk club but* Move
Your Body *was a track that I could play and mix in and it
would always work. I then started to introduce other House
tracks and that worked with the crowd too. It even got those
people that were resistant to change.*

Move Your Body *really got my attention and after that
Trax Records was the label to keep an eye on. It was Marshall
that introduced a lot of people in the UK to Trax and that
Chicago scene. Marshall was an innovator and it was him that
put House music on the map for us.* Someday *was a song that
gave us hope. That and Joe Smooth's* Promised Land *had
messages of hope and were big for us back then.*

Colin Hudd.

In 2013 I got involved with Virus J and Dirty Orkestra who
made up the group House Of Virus. We did *Low Down/Kick
Me a Kick* and *Believe in Love* that featured Soliaris. James
Finnings won me in that contest (a studio session with the

Godfather of House Marshall Jefferson) and, then I got to know his brother Phil and lived in various places with him.

The House of Virus was a concept that James came up with and he approached me about doing some music together. I provided the vocals for the tracks saying stuff like 'let's do the lowdown'. James is a very creative person, very talented and we still have regular contact. The other part of House of Virus was a guy named Justin and he was from Lithuania. He's a very productive person, very task focused, the kind of guy you can tell what you want and he'll figure it out straight away.

In 2013 the producer Matt Tolfrey released a track called *The Truth* featuring Marshall Jefferson. This came out on Leftroom Records. I did the vocals for that song too.

I did a track called *In the Beginning* with Letthemusicplay and UTRB. That was me doing the vocals on that 'once upon a time, back in the day, there were caveman' and I go on to say that they didn't have stereos or TV, they couldn't even talk, they just grunted. And then go on to explain how one day that caveman was sitting on his own and he sees a female passing by and how he got inspired and started to grunt. But because everybody grunted the female didn't take any notice. The caveman then had to think quickly because he wanted to grab the female's attention so he picked up a log and he started beating it. The female heard the sound that the caveman was making and she got curious. Due to her curiosity she walked over to the caveman to see what he was doing. The caveman had a success and that's how House music started. I then get into how House parties started and how other guys started beating on shit too. There's a whole story contained in the song about how the weekend came out.

A couple of years passed by, I mostly just chilled with Shelia and played video games and then I found myself working with Sleezy D. A track called *Do You Believe* was put out under Full Intention and Marshall Jefferson present Sleezy D. Full Intention are two British guys called Jon Pearn and Michael Gray. They're very prolific artists. Sleezy was in the UK so we got together to make the track. We'd stayed in contact all throughout the years of us going our separate ways since the days of those early Chicago club nights. Jon and Michael did the music and I produced the vocals that Sleezy did. It was me who flew Sleezy into the UK so that he could do the vocals.

Sleezy had stayed in Chicago. He'd got married and had three kids but he didn't stay with making music. He'd been working some job but had lost it and that was when I invited him to come to the UK and make a record with me.

It was good to see Sleezy and spend that time with him. In fact it's good whenever I see any of those guys from back in the early Chicago days. I'm still in regular contact with lots of them. I call up Curtis or Byron and we reminisce about the old days. Some things about our lives have remained the same and other things, like chasing women, have changed. But when I talk to my boys it makes me feel closer to home and I appreciate that.

I think the guys and me generally look back on those early Chicago House music days fondly. I believe we all shared similar experiences relating to the songs that came out and going to the clubs like the Music Box and the Warehouse and those experiences shaped who we have become as men. And I think the guys are happy and feel proud to have been part of something that was so special.

Another of those guys from the early days was Steve 'Silk' Hurley and in 2016 we got together to make a track called *Just a Feeling (That I Get)*. We did the song and it featured B. Lauren and that was Steve's daughter. Steve did a fantastic job producing that track. If there's one thing Steve has always had a talent for, it's finishing things and throughout his career he's been prolific with doing that.

The track came about because Steve called me up and asked if I'd like to do a track. I said sure and I spent about twenty minutes coming up with the music. I then sent Steve the track and he took it from there.

Just a Feeling (That I Get) was the last song I made. Making music just isn't at the forefront of my mind these days. At my home I have some equipment but I don't have a set-up that's ready to be making music for a certain level.

To be honest I don't know if I miss making music just for my own pleasure. Music is still a massive part of my life. I'm playing out most weeks and I listen to music all the time. I guess if I felt the urge to make some music I would just jump on my computer and make some.

Other people have continued to make songs using my music. Joey Negro approached saying he wanted to do something together and we tried. He had done a mix of *Ride the Rhythm* and *Raindance* so I said okay and we agreed to get together. I had first met Joey (real name Dave Lee) back in the

90s and by then he was already a very prolific guy. He went on to have some big hits with Jakatta like *American Dream*. The opportunity came up for us to work together and I went to stay with him and his wife. We tried to do something together but we just couldn't come up with anything. Joey has a nice studio set-up at his home and we spent three days trying to make a song but it just didn't happen. I guess I just didn't come up with anything that Joey liked.

The thing is when I'm working on a song people sometimes only hear part of it. The part that is unfinished and they kind of give me a look that says they don't think too much about it. But this is because they haven't heard the finished work. It's been like that since my days when I was making *Move Your Body*. I think this is what happened with the Joey situation – I didn't get to the finish line.

Maybe Joey expected me to come up with a song like *Move Your Body* or *Ride the Rhythm*, but in my mind I had come up with something even better than those songs, it's was just that Joey wasn't hearing it like I was.

Of course *Move Your Body* is the song that people know me for. In 2012 I recorded it with Curtis because Benny Benassi did a mix of it. It was released as Benny Benassi VS Marshall Jefferson. Ultra Music was behind the record. I had signed up with the label in 2009. They were a label based in New York who had put out music from the likes of Sasha, John Digweed and David Guetta. At the time of Ultra contacting me about Benny Benassi wanting to remix *Move Your Body* I didn't even know who he was. I mean there were so many producers out there making music.

But Benny did his thing with the song and it took off. A video was made to accompany *Move Your Body* and that got a thumbs-up from me. It was basically footage of a bunch of kids dancing to the song, but the video did help reach a generation of people that perhaps hadn't been around back in 86 when *Move Your Body* had first been released.

This was also only my second video for one of my songs. There had been a video made back in the 90s for *Find the Groove* but it hadn't taken off like the Benny video had.

Videos are common now, labels know they need a good video to help promote and sale the song. The way the music-buying public has changed too and the record labels understand this and so are always moving quickly to stay ahead. Some people say kids that go clubbing are just more interested in looking good and looking cool and are not paying attention to the music, but I don't necessarily agree with that way of thinking.

I agree that the whole music industry is fucked up. That's inevitable when there are over a hundred thousand songs coming out all the time. I mean that's every week. It used to be only something like fifty dance records coming out a week and that would be the maximum number. When it was like that you could keep up with the new music coming out but nowadays so much gets lost and that's a pity because there's probably some really hot music being made. So we now have a situation where they are a hundred thousand songs coming out this week that are already competing with the hundred thousand that came out the previous week and that's why it's fucked up, and that's why there aren't any more hits.

What I would like to see happen is an act come up from the underground. Dance music has always been the most popular music and that's because people like to dance. The 1920s had its particular dance music, the 1930s and 1940s and so on through the decades – every generation has its thing. What this current generation needs is its own thing and an underground act to ignite it. The situation at the moment is that dance music has lost its power because it's become too separated. It's no longer unified. I'd like to see something change that shakes the industry up.

The major labels have a level of control that stifles creativity. They only want acts that have good-looking people in it because they know they can promote that and so that leaves people thinking that's what they want and need. And that's why you have the likes of Justin Bieber in the industry. So yeah, I would like to see a new underground act come up and present a new genre and flip-flop everything over.

But for me what's next is retirement. I don't even know if I would miss the touring and travelling. I've been doing it for over thirty years. I look forward to being able to retire and just chill. I would probably leave the UK too and go and live with Sheila and the kids in New Jersey. England has been a wonderful place to live and I'm glad that I have been able to spend so much of my life living here and I would miss it, but going back to the States is what I would need to do and where I would need to be and that's where I would write my next chapter from.

MARSHALL MUSIC

This is not an exhaustive list of Marshall's music but there's plenty here for you to get your teeth into.

- *Ride The Rhythm* – Marshall Jefferson. 1986. Trax Records TX105
- *I've Lost Control* – Sleezy D. 1986. Trax Records TX113
- *Free Yourself/Under You* – Virgo. 1986. Trax Records TX114
- *The House Music Anthem (Move Your Body)*. Marshall Jefferson. 1986. TX117
- *Ride the Rhythm* – On The House. 1986. Trax Records TX121
- *The Jungle*-Jungle Wonz. 1986. Trax Records TX129
- *Time Marches On* – Jungle Wonz. 1987. Trax Records TX135
- *Give Me Back The Love* – On The House. 1987. Trax Records TX136
- *Lost in the Groove* – Hercules. 1987. Trax Records TX152
- *Let's Get Busy* – Curtis McClaine and Marshall Jefferson. 1988. Trax Records TX159
- *Do The Do* – Dancing Flutes. 1988. Underground Records

- *Open Your Eyes* – Marshall Jefferson PresentsTruth. 1988. Big Beat
- *Do the Do/Tees Revenge* – Dancing Flutes/Tyree. 1988. Westside Records
- *We Are Unity* – Umosia. 1990. Other Side Records
- *Message to Ron* – Club MCM. 1992. Rhythm Beat
- *Needs (Not Wants)* – Mood Life. 1993 Strictly Rhythm
- *Sunshine N' Your Eyes* – Marshall Jefferson. 1994. Interstate Records
- *I Found You* – Marshall Jefferson. 1994. Centrestage Records
- *Far Behind* – Idle and Wild. 1994. Hot Records
- *Jump On It* – Marshall Jefferson. 1995. KTM/Other Side Records
- *Step by Step* – Marshall Jefferson and Curtis McClaine. 1995. Freetown Inc
- *Mushrooms* – Marshall Jefferson and Noosa Heads. 1996. Soar Records
- *Day of the Onion* – Marshall Jefferson. 1996. KTM
- *12 Inches of Love* – Marshall Jefferson and Jesse Saunders. 1996. Just Say House
- *Vertigo* – Marshall Jefferson/ Think By Divine. 1996. Power Records
- *Touch The Sky* – Marshall Jefferson. 1996. Fifty First Records
- *Animals* – Marshall Jefferson. 1997. KTM
- *I Got Da Feeling* – Marshall Jefferson. 1997. Strawberry Records

- *One More Chance* – Marshall Jefferson/Jesse Saunders featuring Farley 'Jackmaster' Funk. 1998. VCA Records
- *Clap Your Hands* – Marshall Jefferson and DJ Pierre. 2001. DJP Records
- *Music Makes Me Happy* – Marshall Jefferson. 2001. Cleveland City Records
- *69%* – Marshall Jefferson and Serge Imhof. 2002. Onephatdeeva.
- *Coffee 2 Go* – Fuf & Goz. 2003. Kinky Vinyl
- *Feel Me* – Marshall Jefferson featuring Rachael Pearson. 2005. USB Records
- *Colours* (part 1 and part 2). Marshall Jefferson. 2006. USB Records
- *Raindance* – Ragtyme featuring Byron Stingily. 2009. 2 Records
- *Mind and Soul* – Fabio Testi. 2009. Look At You Records
- *Party People* – Todd Terry. 2011. Henry ST. Music
- *We Groove You* – Harley and Muscle. 2012. Soul Star
- *Low Down/Give Me A Kick* – House of Virus. 2013. Skint
- *In the Beginning* – Let The Music Play. 2014. Junk Dog Records
- *Do you Believe* – Full Intention and Sleezy D. 2016. Freakin 909
- *Just a Little Feeling (That I Get)* – Steve Silk Hurley. 2016. Sands Records

Marshall Jefferson albums:
Marshall Jefferson: This Is Other Side Records 1994
- *Red Light, Green Light* – Spatial Understanding
- *Bigger Than Life* – All For Love
- *Stay Up* – Party Girls

- *Mr Groove* – Vicki Ryan
- *Missing You* – Eleven
- *Rock-A-Bye-Baby* – Spatial Understanding
- *The Way I Feel* – Musical Expression
- *My Life to Live* – Two Meanings
- *High And Mighty* – Bigger Than Life

The Definitive Story: Marshall Jefferson. Chicago 86-91
- 1.Marshall Jefferson – *Move Your Body*
- 2. Farley Jack Master Funk – *Love Can't Turn Around*
- 3. Terry Baldwin – *Housemaster*
- 4. Phuture – *Acid Trax*
- 5. Kevin Irving – *Children of the Night*
- 6. Adonis – *No Way Back*
- 7. Mr Lee – *Come To My House*
- 8. Housemaster Boys – *House Nation*
- 9.Curtis McClain – *Let's Get Busy*
- 10. Sleazy D – *Lost Control*
- 11. Jungle Wonz – *Bird in a Guilded Cage*
- 12. Ralphi Rosario Featuring Xavier Gold – *U Used to Hold Me*

Side two:
- Mr Fingers – *Can You Feel It*
- Screamin' Rachel – *The Real Thing (Carl Bias Mix)*
- Kevin Irvine – *Ride The Rhythm*
- Jungle Wonz – *The Jungle*
- Maurice – *This is Acid*
- Hercules – *Lost in the Groove*

- Frankie Knuckles – *Your Love*
- Paris Grey – *Don't Make Me Jack*
- Phuture – *Your Only Friend*
- Phortune – *String Free*
- Jesse Valez – *Girls On The Floor*
- Robert Owens – *Bringing Down The Walls*

Side three: Marshall Jefferson the original house innovator delivers a classic mix of the truly legendary tracks which define the sound of Chicago.

Welcome to the World of Marshall Jefferson (A Testament To House Music) 2001

Side one:

Mr Fingers – *Can You Feel It*
- Jaydee – *Plastic Dreams*
- Marshall Jefferson – *The Cow*
- Mood Life – *Needs Not Wants*
- Robert Owens – *I'll Be Your Friend*
- Photon Inc – *Generate Power*
- Alison Limerick – *Where Love Is*
- Marshall Jefferson – *Move Your Body*
- Adonis – *No Way Back*
- Bam Bam – *Give It To Me*
- Farley 'Jackmaster' Funk – *Trax U Lost*
- Master C & J – *When You Hold Me*
- Sweet D – *Thank Ya*

Side two:

- Kings of Tomorrow – *Finally*
- J Majik feat. Kathy Brown – *Love Is Not A Game*

- Delicious Inc – *Love Me Or Leave Me*
- Foreal People – *Gotta Thing*
- Bel Amour – *Rhythm Master Mix*
- Jesse Saunders – *Body Music*
- Massimo Lippoli Les Hommes – *Indispensable*
- Marshall Jefferson VS Noosa Heads – *Mushrooms*
- Telly Bi. Giordan Mind – *Star Dance*
- Will Bates – *All U Gotta Do Is Love Me*
- X-Press 2 – *Muzikizum (part one)*
- Paul Johnson – *I Ain't Got No Soul*
- Demetrios feat. Ana – *Celebrate*
- Raw Essence feat. Maxine McClain – *Do You Love What You Feel*

Move Your Body: The Evolution of Chicago House. 2003
Side one:
- Pockets – *Come Go With Me*
- Logg – *You've Got That Something*
- Issac Hayes – *I Can Turn Around*
- Inner Life – *I'm Caught Up (In a One Night Love Affair)*
- First Choice – *Let No Man Put Asunder*
- Cheryl Lynn – *You Saved My Day*
- Frankie Knuckles feat. Jamie Principle – *Your Love*
- Mr. Fingers – *Can You Feel It*
- Nightwriters – *Let The Music Use You*
- Fingers Inc. – *Mysteries Of Love*
- Jungle Wonz – *Time Marches On*
- Serious Intention – *You Don't Know*
- Peech Boys – *Don't Make Me Wait*
- Phuture – *Acid Tracks*
- Sleezy D – *I've Lost Control*

Side two:
- E.S.G – *Moody*
- Adonis – *No Way Back*
- Joe Smooth – *Promised Land*
- Quest – *Mind Games*
- Marshall Jefferson – *Move Your Body*
- Ten City – *Devotion*
- Phortune – *String Free*
- Ce Ce Rogers – *Someday*
- Ralph Rosario feat Xavier Gold – *You Used To Hold Me*
- Hercules – *7 Ways To Jack*
- William S – *I'll Never Let You Go*
- Farley 'Jackmaster' Funk – *Love Can't Turn Around*
- Chip E – *Like This*
- Inner Life feat. Jocelyn Brown – *Ain't No Mountain High Enough*

My Salsoul: Foundations of House. 2004
Side one:
- *Are You Single* – Aurra
- *High* – Skyy
- *Hit and Run* – Loleatta Holloway
- *I Got My Mind Made Up* – Instant Funk
- *Moment of my Life* – Inner Life
- *My Love is Free* – Double Exposure
- *Double Cross* – First Choice
- *Love Sensation* – Loleatta Holloway
- *You're Just The Right Size* – The Salsoul Orchestra

- *Doctor Love* – First Choice
- *Just As Long As I Got You* – Love Committee
- *Ain't No Mountain High Enough* – Inner Life

Side Two:
- *Everyman* – Double Exposure
- *First Time Around* – Skyy
- *Sing Sing* – Gaz
- *Ooh I Love It (Love Break)* – The Salsoul Orchestra
- *Call Me* – Skyy
- *Jingo* – Candido
- *Thousand Finger Man* – Candido
- *Law and Order* – Love Committee
- *Love Is You* – Carol Williams
- *Salsoul Rainbow* – The Salsoul Orchestra
- *Crying*-Instant Funk
- *Hold Your Horses* – First Choice
- *Catch Me on the Rebound* – Loleatta Holloway

CPSIA information can be obtained
at www.ICGtesting.com
Printed in the USA
BVHW031835210619
R10044300002B/R100443PG551532BVX10B91/P81788 303989